AZARIAH
OF DORNAKAL

AZARIAH OF DORNAKAL 1874–1945

AZARIAH

OF DORNAKAL

BY CAROL GRAHAM

S.C.M. PRESS LTD
56 BLOOMSBURY ST., LONDON, W.C.1

TO MRS. AZARIAH
in Loving Remembrance

First published May 1946

Distributed in Canada by our exclusive
agents, The Macmillan Company of
Canada Limited, 70 Bond Street, Toronto

Printed in Great Britain by Northumber-
land Press Limited, Gateshead-on-Tyne

CONTENTS

ACKNOWLEDGEMENTS

ᴛ would have been impossible to write this memoir of Bishop Azariah without the help, most generously given, of his many friends and admirers in India, England and America. I would like especially to thank Mrs. Azariah, the Bishop of Worcester and Dr. Sherwood Eddy for material supplied; Bishop and Mrs. Whitehead and Bishop Stephen Neill for their help over the early days in Tinnivelly and Madras and the foundation of the Dornakal Diocese; Miss Doggett for her reading of the manuscript and for many valuable suggestions; and the Archbishop of Canterbury for so kindly allowing me access to the records of the Lambeth Conference. Of necessity, in a book of this compass, much has been curtailed or omitted, and on much the verdict of history remains to be written; but, such as it is, it is offered in deepest affection and respect to the memory of one who was a most true and beloved Father-in-God.

CAROL GRAHAM

Charminster
February 1946

FOREWORD

I AM glad to be given this opportunity of recommending this book on the life and work of Bishop Azariah of Dornakal. It gives an interesting and moving description of the character and activities of one of the most remarkable of recent bishops of the Anglican Communion. It is a book which should be found in every missionary library, and should be read by all who are interested in the extension of Christ's Kingdom overseas.

At the Tambaram Conference at the end of 1938 I had many conversations with the Bishop. Like all who came into contact with him, I was deeply impressed with his quiet grace and humility, which were combined with unflinching determination and deep wisdom. He rarely spoke at the full meetings of the Conference, though, when he did so, he was listened to with the greatest attention. But his influence was felt mainly in committee work and in informal talk with delegates who had come from all parts of the world. None of us who were present will ever forget that Christmas morning when he celebrated the Holy Communion assisted by Bishops from Africa, China, Japan, America and Great Britain, and gave the sacred Food to men and women of all races.

He had three great aims : First and foremost, the conversion of the people of India to Christ. In the mass movement he saw and used the great opportunity for evangelization. He inspired the Indians he baptized with the missionary spirit so that they, in turn, became agents for spreading the Kingdom of Christ. But he never sacrificed quality to numbers, and always insisted on careful preparation and instruction before baptism. Secondly, as the first Indian to be consecrated Bishop in the Anglican

Communion, he was convinced that the faith must be presented in terms, and worship conducted in a manner, most natural and intelligible to the people of India. Worship in Western forms is foreign and strange to the Asiatic. He encouraged, therefore, the use of Indian customs and tunes in the worship of the Church. His great Cathedral at Dornakal is the outstanding example of the adaptation of Indian art to Christian worship. And, thirdly, he was a protagonist in the cause of re-union. His experience made it plain to him that a divided Christendom was unlikely to make much impression against united Hinduism. It was on account of his passionate conviction that it was our Lord's will that His disciples should be one that he threw himself into the advocacy of the South India Scheme.

Those who read this book will be able to understand something of the enthusiasm and devotion of a great Christian leader, who was a true Father-in-God, a shepherd of his sheep, and who in his own life showed forth the beauty and attractiveness of holiness.

CYRIL EBOR

February 1946

I. HAIL

It is the year of our Lord 1943 in India. The Viceroy has resigned and there is the usual speculation as to who will succeed him. A group of Indians and Europeans are discussing the possibility, remote indeed but still a possibility, that an Indian might be appointed to the highest office in their own country. But who? Various names, well known in the political world, are suggested and turned down by one or another. Then somebody says : " There is one man in India who could do it, Azariah of Dornakal, but they would never have the sense to choose him ! " And there was no dissentient voice. In India, torn by communal bitterness, divided by racial and religious barriers, rent asunder by political strife, there is apparently one man about whose powers of statesmanship, qualities of greatness and devotion to India most thinking men would, in their heart of hearts, agree; and yet to many thousands of people in England his name is hardly known. Who and what was Azariah of Dornakal?

The sun is setting over a typical scene in the Telugu country of South India. Against the clear, pale sky of eventide lies a range of forest-covered hills, mysteriously blue and purple in the softening light. In the foreground is a wide valley, standing so thick with the tall, golden crop of ripening corn that, as the evening breeze ripples through the heavy ears, it does indeed appear to laugh and sing. Here and there small lakes, fringed with palm trees and surrounded by high banks, show how precious is every drop of water that flows down from the hills. Clumps of dark trees dotted about show where there are villages and villages and yet more villages, some of them big centres of rural life, others little more than hamlets

where mud huts are roughly huddled together. Along innumerable narrow footpaths the village folk are wending
their way homewards after the day's work; men, lightly
clad in unbleached homespun, smoking the rolled up
tobacco leaf; women, in bright-coloured saris, carrying
their sickle-shaped knives; girls, balancing full earthen-
ware water-pots on their heads with perfect ease; very
small boys driving enormous ungainly buffaloes. And
over all broods the peace of the day's end.

After being practically deserted all day, the villages are
coming to life. There is a bustle of pounding and grinding
before the evening meal. Children are everywhere, dart-
ing in and out in their brown birthday suits, with the
scantiest bits of odd clothing, or none at all. A few are
having their daily bath, standing outside on a convenient
stone while mother or grandmother pours the water over
them. As the sun slips down behind the hills, the blue
smoke wreathing up into the clear air and the acrid smell
of the village fuel proclaim that cooking has begun. When
darkness falls the simple meal is ready. Then, as the
moon rises full and golden, bathing the whole landscape
with its brilliant light, almost imperceptibly, as if by
magic, a crowd has gathered in the village street, men,
women, children, babies, sitting on the ground in a mood
of tense expectancy. In the midst, perched on the edge of
a rock, is a man dressed in simple Indian garb, as perfectly
at home with them as they are with him. For as he speaks
to them, using only the simple idiom of the village, it is
obvious that he holds them in the hollow of his hand, not
by the force of emotional rhetoric, but by shrewd, persuasive argument, driving in his points with homely illus-
trations and touches of humour that provoke grunts of
approval or ripples of laughter.

And what is it all about? One word gives the answer :
Christ. Somebody once asked Bishop Azariah : " If you
were in a village where they had never heard of Christ
what would you preach about? " And he answered with-

10

out hesitation : " The Resurrection." These words bear the imprint of his lifelong conviction : " The Church's message to the world is the Lord Jesus Christ Himself in all His manifold grace and power. It is the work of evangelism . . . so to exalt and proclaim Him crucified, risen, glorious . . . that men may enter upon a new life of abounding hope for this world and the world to come."

An evangelist ? Yes, and more than an evangelist; for not only was it the consuming passion of his own life to bring others to Christ, but it was his burning conviction that no Church could be true to its Founder, no Christian loyal to his Master, unless witness to Christ were their avowed aim. His famous dictum : " Every Christian a Witness," was far more than a mere slogan; it was the solid aim towards which all his thinking and praying, teaching and planning converged and which he explicitly defined in the following words : " Let us make known to all our people the chief purpose for which the Church exists. Let us not be content until this duty is accepted by every communicant in our congregations. *To be His witness, that is the sole object of our existence as Christians.*"

But so far no mention of Dornakal; where and what is that ? A completely inconspicuous little village in the Deccan; a small railway junction, existing to serve some collieries in the State of Hyderabad; a centre of Christian life and the scene of one of the great romances of the Gospel, so that the mere name quickens the pulses of the initiated in almost every corner of the globe. Let us see it in the stillness of a hot Sunday morning, all the activities of school and lecture room, farm and workshop, enfolded in a Sabbath peace. The simplicity of its cottage buildings with their whitewashed walls and red-tiled roofs form a striking contrast to the beauty and dignity of the great Cathedral in the centre. This unique contribution to Indian Christian architecture, laid out on the pattern of a Hindu temple, with its Dravidian pillars bearing aloft their Christian symbolism, its twin towers with their snow-white domes surmounted by silver crosses soaring far up to meet the dawning day, does indeed proclaim Christ as the fulfilment of the age-long search after God in the ancient religions of India. Passing through the enclosed garden which, true to Indian tradition, guards the peace of God round about His holy temple, we enter the Cathedral by the west door. On a wide expanse of polished floor, innocent of pews, a large congregation has gathered for a very special service. The women, in their coloured festal saris, look like a brilliant mosaic. A group of Indian musicians form a band and lead the singing of the Telugu Lyrics. The sanctuary glows with golden hangings, lighted candles, coloured flowers. In the chancel the Bishop is seated in a golden cope, while before him kneel the men he is ordaining to the priesthood. The ceremonial belongs to the ancient heritage of the Catholic Church. It is carried through with simplicity, reverence and dignity, yet hardly more than a handful of those assembled in the church are more than one, or at the most, two generations removed from the ignorance, dirt and degradation of the Indian outcaste villager.

A Father-in-God? Yes, in the fullest sense of the word. One who loved the Catholic heritage of the Anglican communion, who desired the fullest measure of sacramental life for the Church of India, who put before all else the training of a consecrated Indian priesthood, who longed above all to see India bring her gifts of music and art, worship and devotion to the feet of the King of Kings. It is no coincidence that this great Church was consecrated on January 6th, 1939, as the Cathedral Church of the Epiphany; it is rather a fitting witness to that task of manifesting Christ in all His simplicity and all His glory which has gathered in such a rich harvest of India's love and adoration.

Yet if the life and work of Bishop Azariah were rooted

in the villages of his own beloved Diocese of Dornakal, his influence and manifold activities went far beyond. He was indeed a devoted son of India, and all who sought to win India for Christ were his friends and fellow-workers in the furtherance of the Gospel. As President of the National Christian Council of India for nearly seventeen years, he was acclaimed by all denominations as the foremost Christian leader of India, but was always among them as one that serveth, and travelled unceasingly over enormous distances to place his wisdom and experience at the disposal of a nation-wide Church. 'Indianization', so often narrowed down to a grudging devolution of jealously guarded authority into the hands of Indians, he saw always in terms of what India could give to the glory of God and the manifestation of Christ. When the Anglican Communion in India obtained its independence and became the Church of India, Burma and Ceylon, he hailed it as an opportunity for it to enter more fully into the rich heritage of India's religious past. " The religious spirit of India . . . always unbalanced because it is apart from the full revelation of God in Christ, is still an inheritance that Indian believers must bring into the Church and thereby enrich the expression of its character. This spirit comes not through constitution and legislation, but through the personality of every Indian Christian."

At the same time his was no narrow nationalism, no indiscriminate love of India and things Indian. The sentiment, my country right or wrong, found not the faintest echo in his heart. He saw only too clearly the weaknesses of India and loved her with a strong purifying emotion. Moreover, during a period of increasing tension and mounting racial animosity, he continued unwavering in his appreciation of much that he believed to be fine and staunch in the British character and administration, while seeing equally clearly the failures and shortcomings. He followed his Master in his scrupulous discrimination between the nationalist and the patriot, and was in line with

St. Paul in his respect for the State, in so far as it did not interfere with his higher loyalty as a Christian. He wanted the best that East and West could give, both for his country and for the Church, and the rich blend of the two cultures in his own vision and personality enabled him to be a sympathetic interpreter of one race to the other.

Wider still reach the circles on the deep waters of his life. For the simple congregations of the Telugu villages, the Church in the Diocese of Dornakal, the fellowship of Christian believers in India, must be loved and cherished, chastened and purified, not for themselves alone, but in their relation to the One, True, Holy, Catholic fellowship of an undivided Christendom. The Bishop never thought or spoke in terms of ' reunion '; his was not the limited aim of a mere healing of sectarian breaches, although admittedly that was a necessary beginning. The vision for which he prayed and worked, thought and planned with every breath of his whole being, was that of a world-wide Church, wholly united in its allegiance to Christ, strong in its witness to the Christian way of life, definite in its devotions, ordered in its ministry, rooted in sacrament and prayer, comprehensive in the expression of its worship. This was the end for which he worked so patiently and hopefully in South India. This was the message he proclaimed so eloquently and the cause he pleaded so earnestly at Lambeth, Lausanne and Edinburgh, basing it not primarily on the urgent, practical need for union (though that was never far from his thoughts), but on the appalling sin of disunion, the rents in the seamless robe of our Lord. "Such an ideal alone is worth our prayers, efforts and sacrifices. Such alone will prove to the world the reality and power of the Christian faith. *This alone will meet the heart-searching of our Blessed Lord.*"

But when all is said and done about his life and work it is the man himself who remains. How bring back to

14

life that vivid, joyous, dynamic, lovable personality, that delightful humour, that irresistible charm? There are certain things which stand out as an index to his character and help to delineate this great Christian of our generation. First, his unerring instinct for going to the root of any matter and seeing it in a spiritual perspective. It seemed impossible for him to see anything in a trivial light, to discuss any matter without bringing his whole heart and mind to bear upon it. In all the subjects which he made so peculiarly his own, Evangelism, Union, the Indian Church, Christian Giving, Christian Marriage, he could never be satisfied with any superficial thought, any compromise with a lower ideal, any motives of expediency. He had to probe each to its depths, see it in the light of God's will, work out its spiritual implications and then bear witness to the results. He was not a great orator, but the speeches which he made and the sermons which he preached on great occasions all show evidence of this deep balance of thought between the spiritual and the practical, and an eloquence born of simple, direct and almost passionate sincerity.

Secondly, he had a vital interest in people rather than in things or places which, as a rule, gave him a clear insight into those with whom he had to deal. He could suffer fools patiently if not gladly; he had no use whatever for pose or pretence. To make a mistake was easily forgivable; to attempt to justify oneself for having done so was inexcusable. For those who found themselves chafing under an outspoken reproof it was a salutary exercise to probe beneath the surface resentment and find that the Bishop had laid his finger unerringly upon a weakness of character or an unconfessed sin. Was he an autocrat, as some have averred? Call him rather a disciplinarian, remembering always that he began with himself for, as has been truly said of him : " He regarded indiscipline as the breeding ground of sin." By his own life spent utterly to the point of exhaustion in the service

15

of the Master, he earned the right to demand the highest of all who served under him, and his standard was indeed almost terrifyingly high and yet so deeply human in its application as to seem almost easy.

Thirdly, he had a fine inner humility, not always apparent to those who knew him least, but nevertheless very real. He wrote to a friend concerning *Humility, the Beauty of Holiness*, by Andrew Murray : " Next to the Bible this book has helped me most in my Christian life. . . . It humbles any genuine Christian, but that is exactly what is wanted. The more one feels the ideal is far from one's experience, the more one is compelled to cast oneself on God." That is undoubtedly a revealing glimpse of his inner experience, for his dominant personality, his emphatic assurance concerning the things he held most dear and his frank enjoyment of appreciation concealed a deep lowliness of heart which found expression in his favourite text : By the grace of God I am what I am. No man of his calibre and position could have been universally popular, least of all in India, and cheap popularity was the last thing he sought. On one occasion, when a particularly unjust article had been written in a somewhat unsavoury local newspaper, he remarked that it had driven him to meditate upon the text : Woe unto you when all men shall speak well of you.

Another characteristic was his eagerness to learn wherever he went. A visit to the great Brahmo-Samaj training institute at the source of the Ganges revealed methods which he delighted to think could be adapted for Indian Christians; another visit to some Brahmin schools brought him home full of ideas for securing greater reverence in worship among the school-children at Dornakal. It was at a service at St. Giles' Cathedral, Edinburgh, that he first saw the bread and wine for the Communion brought in as part of the people's offering, and years later he instituted this as a feature of the service in Dornakal Cathedral. Wherever he went he looked for inspiration and received it because his mind was alert to use everything for the glory of God.

He allowed himself hardly any relaxation, yet there are few people who knew more of the joy of life. He loved all the little homely courtesies and was deeply touched by signs of affection. One of his guests at Dornakal, who came from a remote village in Dorset, recalls how he put up a picture of Salisbury Cathedral over her bed lest she should feel homesick ! His simple, happy family life, with children and grandchildren, was a joy to be shared freely with all who chose to come. No one could stand on his dignity with him for long; too often you found yourself being led gently ' up the garden path ' with an awful solemnity only belied by an irrepressible twinkle ! And that most lovable smile ! Will anyone who knew him ever forget it ?

It goes without saying that behind the fire and the power, the work and the discipline, the love and the courtesy lay the deep inner sanctuary where God called and he made answer. Faith, humility, piety, devotion, these were the strong, simple virtues which enshrined his inmost life. Prayer was the very mainspring of his existence; the ordered worship of the Church was his delight; the sacraments and the Word of God were the very bread of life. The type of mysticism so often associated with Eastern races did not appeal to him. It was the searching of the Scriptures, enriched by scholarship and devotion, and issuing in an ever deeper consecration of body, mind and spirit from which he drew his daily inspiration and which filled his every need. At home or abroad, in camp or on the move, seldom did he fail to rise at four-thirty to keep his tryst with God. All through his life it was in these quiet hours before dawn that he gained his reserves of strength which enabled him, in the broad noon-day of his maturity, to run without being weary and, in the evening of his life, to walk and not faint.

His own words written in 1937 sum up best that by

which he lived. " My own life has been revived and nourished mainly by two factors, perhaps by three. First, I shall put down the *study* of Holy Scripture. I underline *study*. By this I mean a study, with some authoritative guide or guides, of a book of the Old or New Testament. . . . The effect of such a study is that it turns you away from yourself, delivers you from introspection and places your heart and mind on God. Secondly, I shall put down the Sacrament of Holy Communion. . . . It places your heart and soul on the finished work of Christ. It saves you from any temptation to go far away from the Cross and Resurrection—objective facts which constitute the starting-points of our Christian life. Whatever my feeling may be, or grasp of realities at any particular moment, whatever my failures may be, my being is immersed in the contemplation of something that happened apart from myself and yet which is the pivot around which my life must move. . . . And this creates in us a dependence upon Another and a humility that are the prerequisites of any growth in the spiritual life. Thirdly, I shall put down service. . . . The call to work comes out of the merciful heart of God and is meant to make us feel our nothingness and strive to find by prayer and quiet the strength and purification necessary for the task."

Evangelist, Father-in-God, Apostle of India, Prophet of the world-wide Church. But supremely the man of God, living quite simply in the presence of the heavenly Father until his whole life was shot through and through with God consciousness. And Viceroy? Well, compared with what he was, perhaps that does not seem such a very great destiny after all!

II. THE EARLY YEARS

On the eastern coast of the South Indian peninsula, stretching towards its southernmost tip, lies the district of Tinnively. In the early part of the nineteenth century the countryside looked very much as it does to-day. Stretches of flat, sandy soil, the weird, uncanny shapes of the prickly pear, innumerable palm trees outlined stiffly against the horizon, the brilliant colouring of emerald rice-fields under a blue sky in the tropical sunlight, with flights of white paddy-birds wheeling over them. Women, clad in bright shades of red, blue, orange, work in the fields; men drive the primitive ploughs used by their forefathers from time immemorial; bullock carts creak their way onwards at a snail's pace, the musical tinkle of the bells on the bulls' necks breaking the drowsy midday silence. This is the rural India of the south, unchanged through many centuries and, in most of its essentials, unchangeable.

Here there lived, rather more than a century ago, a poor but very orthodox Hindu family belonging to the Nadar caste, a humble section of Hindu society whose prerogative was the drawing of toddy, the juice which is obtained by tapping the palm trees and which, when fermented, provides the staple strong drink of South India. To ascend the bare trunk of the palm tree to its topmost giddy height and to descend with the pot of precious liquor intact is no mean acrobatic feat and demands a virile people possessed of considerable physical strength and toughness. The fact that they have never possessed the right of entry to the Hindu temples has sometimes led to the misapprehension that they are thus classed with the so-called ' untouchables ', but this is not the case. In

19

recent times, through taking advantage of the education given by Christian missions and the Government, they have proved their ability in many directions and now form an important section of the Church in Tinnivelly.

The head of the family in which we are interested was a grain merchant in a small way, who travelled about with bags of grain and molasses, frequently stopping to make an offering at a wayside shrine or a small gift to someone in need. In 1839 his son, Velayudham, came under the influence of a movement towards Christianity on the part of the Nadar people and ran away to the neighbouring village of Megnanapuram, where he was subsequently baptized under the name of Thomas Vedanayagam, a judicious mixture of the name of the missionary who baptized him coupled with the nearest-sounding Christian equivalent of his old Hindu name. Thomas was educated in the mission school, worked for the mission in the villages steadily and unostentatiously for a quarter of a century, was ordained in 1869 and then completed over twenty years of faithful pastoral ministry, most of which was spent at the little village of Vellalanvillai, where he built the church and is chiefly remembered for his deep spirituality and beautiful reading of the services. He was twice married and by his first wife had a family of two sons and several daughters. His second wife, Ellen, was a lady of deep devotion and great beauty of character. They had one daughter and then, after thirteen years, there was born on August 17th, 1874, the child of many prayers, a son, who was christened Samuel Azariah and, like his namesake in the Old Testament, dedicated from childhood to the service of the Lord.

His early background was one of simple and deep evangelical piety. His mother, with more than the ordinary temptation to spoil him, never even contemplated such a weakness, and certainly one important clue to his character is to be found in the sense of being 'separated unto God' with which he grew up. His father died when he was still a boy, so that his mother became the paramount influence in his life and he never faltered in his steadfast devotion to her. Somebody once stated publicly that Bishop Azariah owed his knowledge of the Bible to his early connection with the Y.M.C.A. " Never," he declared emphatically. " All my love for the Bible and my knowledge of it came to me from my mother." At a conference for boarding-school teachers in Dornakal he was told that the Scripture syllabus he had compiled for children up to the age of fourteen was too full, especially with regard to the amount they had to learn by heart. The Bishop looked nonplussed and protested : " But I knew all those passages by the time I was ten years old ! " In other ways, too, the child was father to the man. When quite a small boy he heard the story of Uganda and the martyrdom of Bishop Hannington. Without a moment's hesitation he took off his new gold bangles and offered them as a gift to Uganda. His school-teacher, thinking it was merely the sudden impulse of emotion, sent him home to get his father's permission. He returned the next day bringing the bangles, and so had his first experience of sacrificial giving for the Kingdom of God. The greatest test of his devotion to his mother and her influence over him came many years later in one of the bitterest decisions of his life. When he was about to sit for his priest's examination in Madras news came from Tinnivelly that his mother was dying. He stayed for the examination and was too late to see her alive, but in relating this many years later to a missionary faced with the same kind of decision he said : " I have never thought I did wrong although she died asking for me."

To return to the little village of Vellalanvillai where his childhood was spent. He attended the village school where the boys learnt to read from palmyra leaf books and traced their alphabet with their fingers on sand. After the death of his father his mother moved into the neighbouring village of Megnanapuram, a big Christian centre with a church whose tall spire was a landmark for many miles around in that flat countryside. At the age of ten Azariah was sent to the boarding-school where sweeping and washing the floor, cooking the school food and watering the garden were accepted as a normal part of the routine. Here we find him, on one occasion, lined up before the veranda of the mission bungalow, one of a row of rather shamefaced little boys being sternly questioned by the missionary's wife concerning the mysterious disappearance of some guavas from the garden. She began by asking, somewhat inadvertently : " Boys, what does the Bible say about thieves ? " to which the eldest and cheekiest little boy replied : " Please, ma'm, ' To-day thou shalt be with Me in Paradise.' " This piece of audacity was not well received, and it was announced that not only the perpetrators of the outrage but all those also who had partaken of the stolen fruit must hold out their hands. This, of course, meant everybody, and the lady went solemnly down the line, caning each in turn, till she came to the last and smallest boy. Here she paused and said with a twinkle in her eye : " I don't think I shall cane you, Samuel Azariah, I shall tell your mother instead." Whereupon the small hand was thrust out still farther and a voice implored : " Oh, please, ma'm, cane me now ; my mother beats much harder than you do." There was no softness in the upbringing of the future leader of the Church.

The headmaster of the school at Megnanapuram, Ambrose Thomas (who was incidentally one of Azariah's step-brothers), was a very remarkable man, a real scholar and a great Christian. The standard of Bible knowledge among his pupils was unknown elsewhere in the East, and many great men owed their instruction in the realities of the Christian faith to him. Azariah has left on record his own tribute. " Many of us are what we are because of his influence, his prayers, his example. Yet there were

22

many days when the time-table was forgotten ; inspiration would make him devote one whole afternoon to Euclid, another to Algebra, again a whole morning to Scripture. These days are gone for ever . . . and with them is passing away the old Guru-Shisya (Master-Disciple) relationship between the teacher and the taught.''

A great art learnt from this same brother, which stood him in good stead in after life, was that of simple translation. For some years Ambrose Thomas spent his leisure in translating Milton into simple Tamil and his practice was to invite an ordinary village man to his house and try out on him the results of his labours. Any word which the villager could not understand at the first reading went out to be replaced by a simpler one. It may have been hard upon Milton, but it remained an indelible memory upon young Azariah's mind, forming in him a nice literary taste which sought always to find expression in the simplest possible style. Many happy hours were also spent in the company of another half-brother who was a printer by trade, and the little boy was proud to earn his first few annas of pocket-money by dusting and sorting the type in the evenings, and so acquired a technical knowledge of printing which was revived many years later when the mission press was set up in Dornakal.

After passing through boarding-school he went to the Church Mission College at Tinnivelly, and it was here that he was instrumental in founding the Christian Brotherhood Association in the hostel for the express purpose of resisting the caste spirit which, alas too often, rears its ugly head even in Christian institutions. In 1893, after a year as a pupil teacher in the C.M.S. High School at Palamcotta, he migrated to the Christian College, Madras, where he joined the B.A. class, and it was here that he adopted the name by which he was to become famous. The Tamil people have no surname and the custom is to use their father's name for this purpose. Accordingly Samuel Azariah had taken the name of Vedanayagam, but on his arrival at college the Principal decided that this was too difficult to remember for everyday use. Yet Samuel was too common, there were already far too many of them. So Azariah he was called and Azariah he remained. His many friends in Western lands may perhaps be thankful for this simplification. After two years at the college he fell ill, on the very day before the examination, and so was unable to take his degree. His education was now finished and life with all its possibilities lay before him, but for him there was only one question : How could he best fulfil his vocation to serve the Lord to whom he had been dedicated from birth ?

This crucial question was answered for him by his being offered the post of secretary to the Y.M.C.A. for South India, which he immediately accepted and occupied for thirteen years. And thus there began for him the first of two great friendships which were destined to influence the whole course of his life. For that very year Sherwood Eddy arrived in India to be the travelling Secretary for the Y.M.C.A. in India and Ceylon. The first Indian he met on his arrival at Calcutta was Azariah, and there began immediately a deep and lasting friendship between them, born of a common evangelistic zeal, cemented by a strong love for India and crowned by the sharing of a common ministry. It was the dawn of the awakening of a new national consciousness in India, a new sense of dignity and independence on the part of Indian Christians, in which such men as K. T. Paul, A. A. Appasamy and V. S. Azariah were eager and ready to take their part. They found in men like Sherwood Eddy and John Mott (who had arrived in India a year or two sooner) kindred spirits of a very rare order, though they little guessed to what extent they were about to make history.

. What did Sherwood Eddy and Azariah chiefly give to one another ? In the first place Eddy opened Azariah's mind to all the treasures of Biblical scholarship which had been revealed by the modern historical method of study-

24

ing the Scriptures. Knowledge and love of the Word of God were already deeply implanted in his heart; now the old truths were floodlit by the new interpretation. Not all of it would stand the test of time, but Azariah had both the faith and the mind which could sift and discern, accept or reject, discard or assimilate this new revelation, and during this more formative period of his life were laid the foundations of up-to-date scholarship, coupled with soundness of faith, which became the hallmark of his inspired Biblical exposition in later days. On the other hand, he was able to give Eddy an insight into the thoughts and feelings, the hopes and aspirations of Indians such as the Westerner usually finds it hard to come by. He was the sincere friend, tactful yet courageous, correcting mistakes, putting him wise in his dealings with students and fellow-workers, Christians and non-Christians, generously, patiently and lovingly interpreting his beloved India to his equally beloved friend. It was not that they consciously tried to influence one another, but they shared, simply and naturally, all they had and all they learned, helping each other to grow in the love and service of God and of India.

There was another more important respect in which this friendship opened a new era in Azariah's life. He had been brought up under the shadow of the early missionaries, many of them giants of old in the scope and extent of their work and second to none in the sacrifice and devotion of their lives. But they were as the fathers and mothers of the young Church which, in many cases, had come to birth within their memory and since, in accordance with the Victorian tradition, children should be seen and not heard in unquestioning obedience, friendship with Indian Christians on equal terms was not normally regarded as a serious possibility. Azariah could and did love and venerate some of the men under whose influence he had grown up, notably the Principals of the two colleges in which he had studied at Tinnivelly and at

Madras, but he had never known what it was to be received into the home of a European on terms of easy familiarity. Quite early in his intercourse with Eddy he hurt him deeply by supposing almost carelessly, when questioned on the subject, that their friendship was as close as it could be between an Indian and a ' foreigner '. When he realized the extent to which Eddy had been wounded by this implied limitation, Azariah was amazed that a Westerner should actually desire so great a degree of intimacy with an Indian. It is hard at this distance to realize the gulf which was then so generally accepted, but it is certain that Azariah was deeply concerned with the whole question of the relationship between missionaries and Indian Christians, and that he played an important part in bringing about a notable change in their regard for one another.

There now passed a decade of arduous and happy service which was to bear great fruit for the future of Christianity in India. Azariah's work lay almost entirely among the younger generation of educated Indian Christians and was predominantly concerned with students. He travelled all over India making endless friends through the charm of his lovable personality, and bringing many to a vivid consciousness of a personal relationship with God. He and his fellow-workers, Indian, American, British, were all young and ardent together, and their aim was nothing less than the conversion of the world in their generation. They carried on a crusade throughout the schools and colleges of India by means of which they sought to build up a generation of Christians on fire with the love of Christ, to raise up Indian leaders for the evangelization of their own land, to arouse in all Indian Christians a true missionary zeal and a passion for unity, so that ultimately they might create an India which, through undivided allegiance to Christ, might take her rightful place in the new world order for which they all worked and prayed. As the Churches of India began to awake to this great challenge the time seemed ripe. for the organization of an interdenominational missionary society that could appeal to all sections of the Christian community for the evangelization of their own country. So, on Christmas Day 1905, in Carey's historic library at Serampore, the National Missionary Society of India was launched by a group of Indian leaders, with Azariah as its first general secretary. To quote their own statement issued at the time : " With Indian men, Indian money and Indian management . . . founding no new denomination, but preserving the strongest loyalty to the Churches, soliciting no funds outside India, but laying the burden of India's evangelization upon her own sons, we believe the Society is organized upon a safe and sound basis. Only after months of careful planning and after securing the approval of hundreds of representative Indians and European missionaries was this important step taken."

So Azariah learnt to plan and to organize, to lead and to co-operate, with a wide vision, unbounded courage and sanctified common sense. He worked prodigiously and read, as he worked, unceasingly and unsparingly. Seldom was he seen, on train or boat, on a long journey or in odd moments, without a book in his hand. His lifelong habits of self-discipline, early rising, simple living, methodical work and unstinting self-giving were all formed in this period. Prayer was as natural and as necessary to him as eating or sleeping. After nearly fifty years Sherwood Eddy has summed up his recollection of him as follows : " Azariah had the gift of a sunny, happy, normal disposition, never solemn or ascetic, with a fine balance between the mystical, devotional and personal aspects of religion on the one hand, and the rational, critical and social aspects on the other. . . . Deep spirituality and deep humility were combined with sagacity and good judgment. . . . He had a passion for unity, harmony and reconciliation ; indomitable faith in God, in man, in India and her future. He was a radiant

27

optimist, always ready for sacrifice without the least touch of asceticism. . . . Tireless in energy and in the organization of his life, always ' redeeming the time ', I never knew him to spend the fraction of an hour without reading or prayer. . . . But most of all I loved him for his utter frankness and sterling integrity."

In 1907 Azariah's horizon was widened by a visit to Japan for a meeting of the World's Student Christian Federation at Tokyo, where he met Christian leaders of other countries and races, and was himself recognized as a spiritual force to be reckoned with in the future. Two years later he became vice-chairman of the Federation, and it did indeed seem as if his course were set for a life of international and interdenominational Christian service in which he was likely to carry all before him. But God moves in a mysterious way, and it was by a more devious and sacrificial path that he was destined to fulfil his vocation and become a Christian leader of world-wide significance.

III. THE INDIAN EVANGELIST

It is now necessary to go back a few years and trace what eventually came to be the most important thread in Azariah's life. We have seen the horizon gradually widening before him; the Madras Presidency, South India and Ceylon, the whole stretch of his native land, Japan and the world outside. His influence among Indian Christians was already remarkable; he was becoming a figure in international and interdenominational Christian circles; he was one of a group who were destined to make history in the world-wide Church. Yet the ties with his own beloved Tamil country had never weakened. There was the Church in which he had been born and bred among the people he knew and loved. Above all there was his home.

In 1898 his thought had turned towards marriage, and there were certainly plenty of Christian parents who would gladly have secured so promising a young man as a *parti* for their daughters. In those days opportunities for young men and women to meet in a friendly way and fall in love were negligible, and even the limited freedom enjoyed to-day amongst young educated Indians of good family would have been looked upon askance. Marriage arrangements in India are still primarily a family concern, the question of a suitable dowry plays an important part, and the personal preference of bride or bridegroom often comes a bad second. In spite of which, when all is said and done, the percentage of happy marriages in India compares favourably with any Western country! But Azariah knew quite well what he wanted, nothing less than " the most spiritually minded girl in Tinnivelly ", and what is more he succeeded in finding her. Miss Anbu

Mariammal Samuel was one of the first Indian Christian women in Tinnivelly to take a college course, and one of still fewer who achieved the old F.A. degree. This she did out of her own quiet determination, since her father held the orthodox views of those days with regard to the unsuitability of higher education for women which had certainly not yet become an asset in the marriage market. But Anbu was no mere blue-stocking, still less a militant advocate of women's rights. Her dominant desire, even then, was to serve the Kingdom of God, and her purpose in continuing her education was simply to fit herself for greater usefulness. She was serious minded, loved simplicity to the verge of asceticism, and already showed much of the promise that was to blossom in later years.

She was betrothed to Azariah in April 1898 and he gave her a Bible as an engagement present. From then on they corresponded and he shared with her his inmost thoughts and aspirations. "Shall I pass on to you what I had this morning in my Bible reading? 'He saved others, Himself He cannot save.' Yes, it is *cannot*, for it was morally impossible to save Himself and others. Seeking pleasure, ease, comfort, luxury—souls *cannot* be saved at the same time, one must give way to the other. What shall be mine? Yours?" There could be but one answer to this. His future bride was completely one with him in all his high-hearted missionary endeavour, sharing to the full his passion for souls. They were married on St. Peter's Day, June 29th, 1898, and never were two people more truly one in mind and spirit, work and prayer, faith and hope and aspiration. It was not that he took her unformed and moulded her to the pattern of his love. It was from the first a true partnership, and all through life they grew together, she keeping pace with him, sharing alike his inward spiritual growth and his outward visible responsibilities. To the casual observer she may have appeared quiet, modest, unassuming, perhaps even shy and reserved. To those who knew her best she had

30

the strength of personality, courage of her convictions and steadfast heroic endurance which betoken a life that is hid with Christ in God.

Thus Azariah's home became the very centre of his life, yet how much time he had to spend away from it! Very soon after his marriage he had to go on tour with Sherwood Eddy to Travancore and he wrote to his lonely little bride : " How hard this separation is ! . . . Yet for *His* sake . . ." It was part of the price she knew she must pay when she accepted him, and together, in their generous self-sacrifice, they never shirked these partings, although even twenty-four hours at home, snatched between tours or meetings, were infinitely precious as times of deep refreshment. In due course children were born to them, a daughter and two sons. It was another part of the sacrifice that he had so little leisure to enjoy the delights of family life. To the children he was indeed a wonderful apparition for whose return, laden with small presents and sweets, they lived continually in happy expectation, but it was the mother who provided their solid background to life and their sense of security. Later on sorrow came to deepen their faith in God. In 1906 a son was born and died within three months. The following year Mrs. Azariah grieved, as only a mother can, for twins whom she scarcely saw. Finally, three more children, another daughter and two sons, completed the family. Yet all the time, in joy or in sorrow, together or in separation, the Kingdom of God must come first, in the sure and certain belief that only so would the manifold blessings of life be added unto them.

Meanwhile the year 1902 became a turning-point in the history of the South Indian Church and not least of Azariah himself. He had gone with Sherwood Eddy to conduct a mission at Jaffna, in Ceylon, the centre of a big Tamil community domiciled in the northern part of the island. Here he found, actually in being, the ideal that was coming more and more to possess his heart. The

Tamil Christians of Jaffna had a missionary society of their own and were sending evangelists to work among their poorer brethren in India. It smote Azariah to the heart to think that his own beloved Christian community in Tinnivelly, with its wealth of church buildings, church schools and church colleges, had so far given neither their money nor their sons, in any marked degree, for the evangelization of their own people, but had left this supremely important part of the Church's task to foreigners. One night he went out along the seashore to pray, his heart a tumult of shame and longing, shedding bitter tears as he thought of how little Indian Christians were doing to carry out the last charge of their Lord and Master. Out of this travail of soul there came to birth the conviction that he was being called by God to bring home to the Church in Tinnivelly both their failure and their responsibility to carry the knowledge of Christ to their own people, and to inaugurate in South India another such experiment as he had found in Ceylon. It might well seem a task beyond the power of one who had neither men nor money at his disposal, but the certainty that with God all things are possible was the bed-rock of Azariah's existence. So it came about that, on that sandy beach under the shadow of the palm trees, with the incredible loveliness of the moonlit sea before him, there was conceived and dedicated to God a purpose which never wavered and which was to bear fruit beyond his wildest dreams.

As soon as he returned to Tinnivelly Azariah imparted his idea to a few kindred spirits and together they literally prayed it into being. By February 1903 the time seemed ripe for action and they founded the Indian Missionary Society of Tinnivelly. Its avowed principles were : Indian men, Indian money, Indian management; and its intention, to find an area where no other mission was working. No subscription list was sent out, no appeal made for volunteers, yet both men and money were soon

32

available. The most difficult task was to find the un-occupied area. They tried various parts of the Tamil country, going gradually farther afield, until eventually they turned their eyes northwards to the Telugu country where they were told that the south-east corner of the Nizam's dominions might be regarded as virgin soil. On going up to reconnoitre Azariah found sixty miles of jungle into which no missionary had as yet penetrated, and where there were only seven Christians all told. He hastened back to lay the project before the Bishop of Madras and this brought him to the second great friendship which was to have so great an effect upon his life.

Henry Whitehead became Bishop of Madras in 1899, just when the urge for a greater measure of freedom and self-government within the Church was springing up in South India. He was a man of deep sympathy with Indian aspirations and wide vision for the future of the Indian Church. He found himself in charge of an enormous diocese, hopelessly unwieldy in extent and almost impossible for one man to administer. Moreover, at almost the farthest point from the centre, in two stretches of the Telugu country, flourishing mass movements were on foot among the outcastes in the villages which alone would have been enough to occupy his full attention. That he did give them a big place in his heart and a large slice of his time is evident from his diary which tells continually of long arduous tours by bullock-cart or on foot, and visits to remote villages where the Church was springing into existence. It was obvious that his primary need was for an Assistant Bishop, and there were many European missionaries of ability and distinction who could have filled such a post. But the Bishop's dream was for an Indian and he preferred to wait, overworked as he was, until, in God's good time, the right man should come to light. And so it was that his prayer was answered and his patience rewarded when, in 1903, Samuel Vedanayagam Azariah arrived in Madras to put before him the project for establishing an Indian mission in the Telugu country.

Their first meeting was in the nature of a revelation on both sides. Bishop Whitehead was immensely struck by the depth of Azariah's vision for the Indian Church and the statesmanlike quality of his plans for this new venture. Azariah was both surprised and overjoyed at the deep sympathy with which his proposal was accepted and the Bishop's entire readiness to recognize the new Society and give a title to the clergy working under it. Complete confidence was therefore established from the outset, and by April 1903 the first missionaries, Samuel Pakkianadan and his brother, were settled in the Telugu country, while Azariah, as the secretary of the Society, was responsible for arousing further interest and collecting the necessary money. The choice of Dornakal as a centre was, in God's providence, a happy accident. They had thought of the Taluq centre, farther up the railway line, but found every conceivable obstacle put in their way by the Mohammedans, who viewed the prospect of a Christian mission in their midst with extreme disfavour. A chance conversation on the station brought to their notice a derelict brewery at the little railway junction of Dornakal and, since this seemed to afford the only available foothold, they jumped at the offer and there they settled down. The missionaries lived at either end, a room in the centre became their chapel, and gradually, as need arose, a school, with dormitories for boys and girls, was also housed under this capacious roof. And so Dornakal began.

The village people among whom their work lay were certainly backward beyond belief. The jungle reached the railway on either side and there were no roads. Even literacy, much less education, was practically unknown. Ignorance, drunkenness and dire poverty from within, oppression and corruption from without, combined to keep the outcastes in a state that was almost sub-human.

The Light of the World burst upon them with a dazzling radiancy, but much time and patience were needed to bring home to them, however simply, the demands of the Way, the Truth and the Life. The first baptism was not until August 3rd, 1906, when Bishop Whitehead baptized twenty-three adults and thirty-three children in the interval between his arrival on one train from Singareni and his departure to Secunderabad on the next. A last minute alteration of the time-table threatened to upset this plan altogether, but by judicious negotiation with the station-master, one train arrived half an hour early and the other left half an hour late ! In addition to those baptized, more than three hundred people were under instruction, and eighteen months later a second baptism reaped the fruits of this slow and careful preparation. The Indian mission had abundantly justified both its existence and its methods, and Bishop Whitehead was greatly impressed and overjoyed at its success.

Azariah, however, was not one who could urge others to go where he himself feared to tread. After a meeting in Madras at which he had been appealing to young Indians for offers of personal service for the evangelization of India, it was suddenly borne in upon him that he must go himself. The casual word of a friend coming just at this moment seemed to him " as the voice of God ", and accordingly he made his decision to offer as a missionary for Dornakal. It was a staggering blow to many of his friends that he should devote his brilliance and his charm, his gifts of statesmanship and his spirituality, to what Sherwood Eddy has termed " the most drunken, degraded, carrion-eating devil-worshippers " in a remote corner of the Hyderabad State and, though they recognized it as a heroic sacrifice, they mourned it as an irreparable loss. But Azariah had no such qualms; where God called he was accustomed to follow. He offered himself to Bishop Whitehead, who accepted him joyfully and advised him to be ordained. The hope that here at

35

last was the answer to his prayers for an Assistant Bishop
had begun to take root.

It was obvious that for anyone so experienced in the
spiritual life and with such a profound knowledge of the
Bible the ordinary theological college would not provide
the kind of training required. Bishop Whitehead therefore invited Azariah to come and read with him, and,
early in 1909, he took up his abode in Madras at Bishop's
House. He loved his reading, and the ensuing discussions
with the older man extended the range and power of his
thought, opened his eyes to the true catholicity of the
Anglican Church and increased his sense of tradition and
order in faith and worship. It was a period of thrilling
expectancy and steady fulfilment on both sides, for
Azariah, who had hitherto rather rejoiced in being something of a free lance, found ever greater satisfaction in
becoming part of the ministry of the Church, and Bishop
Whitehead grew daily more certain that here was a man
who in personality, scholarship, spiritual perception and
general ability was unquestionably fitted to be the first
Indian Bishop. Quite as important to Azariah's development was the rapid ripening of their friendship. He had
already a deep respect for the Bishop's wisdom and saintliness and a real gratitude for his sympathy and help;
now, in the happy informality of home life, their relationship blossomed into a deeply affectionate intimacy without
losing one iota of its reverence. When Azariah first
arrived the Bishop showed him to his room and went
through to the bathroom, remarking that he wished to
see if the servant had remembered to put out soap and
towels. This little act of consideration on the part of an
English Bishop for an Indian so touched Azariah that he
never forgot it and, trivial though it was, it became to
him symptomatic of an intimacy not often found, even
now, between the two races. It was undoubtedly this
happy familiarity and easy intercourse, in which Mrs.
Whitehead also joined, that led Azariah to work for

36

greater freedom and understanding between Indians and
their Western brethren, and to open his own home so
gladly to English and American friends in later years.

Azariah was ordained deacon on St. Peter's Day, 1909,
the anniversary of Bishop Whitehead's consecration and
his own wedding-day. The night before, Bishop Whitehead told him of his hope that he might become the
Assistant Bishop of Madras, so that his ordination took
place under an overwhelming sense of the greatness of his
call and was an act of the deepest submission to the will
of God. Within a month he had taken up work at
Dornakal. His ordination to the priesthood followed in
December of the same year and, early in January, the
whole family migrated to their new home. For an Indian
woman of culture and refinement to uproot herself from
her own people and take a family of young children to
live in the jungle, in the cramped quarters of the old
brewery, knowing that her husband would spend most
of his time away, camping in the villages, called for no
ordinary measure of courage and devotion, but Mrs.
Azariah was at heart a pioneer and a missionary for whom
no demand was too hard, no sacrifice too great. She
followed her husband to the wilds of Dornakal, rejoicing
that she, too, was counted worthy to share in the great
adventure.

Meanwhile Bishop Whitehead had put in train the
machinery for the appointment of an Assistant Bishop.
When the proposal first came before the Episcopal Synod
in 1908 it was received most sympathetically, but when,
two years later, it became known that he proposed to
nominate an Indian, there was an outburst of violent
opposition from many directions. The other Bishops were
extremely doubtful, the English community was horrified,
the Government were dead against it; some missionaries
wrote that they were not willing to serve under an Indian
Bishop and there was jealousy even among Indian Christians. On the other hand, many of the younger genera-

tion, missionaries as well as Indians, hailed it as the opening of a new era in Church policy for which they had been longing. The Metropolitan, Bishop Copplestone of Calcutta, also gave whole-hearted support, and he it was who insisted that the first Indian Bishop should be given an independent diocese, however small, in order to avoid the mischievous conception of an Indian Bishop occupying an inferior position and ministering only to Indian Christians. Even if the worst came to the worst and the vision must tarry for a time, let them work, and wait, and pray for its fulfilment.

Meanwhile, at this critical juncture Azariah had to obey another call. He had been asked by Dr. Mott to attend the World Missionary Conference at Edinburgh in the summer of 1910 and give an address on the problem of " co-operation between foreign and native workers in the younger Churches ". His inclination was to refuse, feeling that he must either suppress the truth under a cloak of hypocrisy or risk inflicting grievous hurt on many who had been his friends. But John Mott was convinced that certain things needed saying and that Azariah was a great enough Christian to say them without rancour, and so he went, obedient as usual to any call that he felt came from God. His speech, which brought him lasting fame, was an eloquent appeal to the missionaries, on behalf of Indian Christian leaders, for friendship on equal terms and the sharing of responsibility on a footing of complete equality. Dr. Mott had asked him to tell out freely and frankly what was on his mind and this he did, speaking under an intense nervous strain, revealing a soreness of heart on the part of Indian Christians and a mounting tension between them and the missionaries which fairly took everyone's breath away and caused many to think furiously. " I do not plead," he said, " for returning calls, handshakes, chairs, dinners and teas as such. I do, on the other hand, plead for all of them and more if they can be expressions of a friendly feeling, if these or

anything else can be the outward proofs of a real willing-
ness on the part of the foreign missionary to show that he
is in the midst of the people to be to them not a lord and
master but a brother and a friend." His peroration, with
its passionate sincerity, still has the power to move deeply
anyone whose heart is with the younger Churches.
" Through all the ages to come the Indian Church will
rise up in gratitude to attest the heroism and self-denying
labours of the missionary body. · You have given your
goods to feed the poor. You have given your bodies to
be burned. We ask also for *love*. Give us *Friends*."

This was throwing the cat among the pigeons with a
vengeance, and Azariah himself said in after years that,
had he the same task to do over again, in the light of
mature experience he might have done it more circum-
spectly. In which case it might have been less effectual !
But the stir it produced in India can easily be understood.
Whether in the long run it made Bishop Whitehead's task
more or less difficult would be hard to say. It probably
hardened the opposition in some quarters. For instance,
one veteran missionary of South India, when, later on,
Azariah was leaving to go to Calcutta for his consecration, remarked gloomily : " I only hope you do as little
harm to the Church of India as you can ! " Yet others,
notably among the younger generation, were filled with
hope that the first Indian Bishop would be both fearless
and revolutionary in his attitude towards the problems
of the Church. In any case, the storm gradually subsided.
The other Bishops came to know more of Azariah and his
work, and to appreciate him at his true worth. Most of
all his bearing under what must have been, to a man of
his outlook, great provocation, his deep submission to the
will of God, whatever it might prove to be, and his true
humility in the face of strong temptation to be otherwise
impressed them greatly. By 1912 most of the opposition
had melted away and the proposal, as originally set forth
by the Metropolitan and Bishop Whitehead, was accepted

in its entirety. Azariah was to be consecrated Bishop of
Dornakal, having under his independent jurisdiction a
small diocese consisting of the Dornakal mission and the
adjoining areas of Khammamett and Singareni, and was
also to act as Assistant Bishop in the Diocese of Madras.

The consecration took place in Calcutta Cathedral on
December 29th, 1912. It was the last public event in
which the Metropolitan took part on the eve of his retirement and he regarded it as the crowning act of his
ministry in India. "Rejoice in the appointment of Indian
Bishops and ask for many more" was his parting advice
to the Indian Church, and he added the timely warning :
"But do not ask for an Indian Bishopric," meaning :
Do not make race distinctions, but look to the time when
Indians can normally and happily preside over Europeans
and vice versa. The Government was represented by the
Governor of Bengal, and all the eleven Bishops took part
in the consecration. John Mott, Sherwood Eddy and
representatives of all denominations were there to support
their friend in this most solemn moment of his career.
The text of the sermon was St. Paul's prayer for the
Church at Ephesus, that, inspired by the Spirit of Christ
within and dominated by the power of His love without,
they might show forth the full beauty of God's love and
God's purpose. How much the future held in common
between the great missionary Apostle of the Church and
the new young Bishop could only have been dimly fore-
seen, yet even then the similarity in their consuming
passion for evangelism and their belief in the witness of
the indigenous Church was striking enough. It was, indeed, a moving moment when the young Indian, clad in
his episcopal robes, knelt before the aged Metropolitan
and other Bishops to receive, by the laying on of hands,
the Apostolic gift which would enable him to take his
place in the long line of those whom God had called to
be the chief Shepherds of His flock. To quote the words
of a Scottish divine, who in later years was to be inti-

mately associated with the new Bishop in many great Christian ventures : " The Anglican Church has done some big and brave things in India, notably in the development of Christian leadership, and among the biggest and bravest I would rank without reservation the appointment of Vedanayakam Samuel Azariah as Bishop of Dornakal."

IV. THE BISHOP OF DORNAKAL

On January 8th, 1913, just ten days after his consecration, the new Bishop was installed in his own diocese. During the intervening days he had taken his place for the first time on the Episcopal Synod, of which he would live to become almost the doyen among the diocesan Bishops. He travelled from Calcutta with Bishop Whitehead, arriving at Khammamett on the evening of January 7th, where they were met by a torchlight procession and led straight to the church, amid scenes of great enthusiasm, for a service of thanksgiving. The following day all the leading Christians of Dornakal and Khammamett were assembled when Bishop Whitehead handed over the new See by commission to Azariah and formally installed him as Bishop of Dornakal. It was a moving moment for the two friends, the fulfilment of such high hopes for the older man, the entering in upon such tremendous responsibilities for the younger.

He certainly brought to his new diocese the freshness and vigour of youth and entered upon his new duties without delay. His first confirmation was held at Dornakal on February 9th, and his first ordination at Khammamett the following Sunday. The area of his diocese was roughly the size of Wales and contained altogether 6 Indian clergy, 172 lay workers and 8,000 Christians. The Dornakal Mission was, of course, his first love, but at Khammamett he found many things after his own heart, notably a very high standard of scriptural knowledge, considerable spiritual progress for so young a Church and a distinctly cosmopolitan flavour, many of the Christians having migrated from the adjoining parts of British India.

From henceforth the Telugu country was to be the land of Azariah's adoption. The name does not stand for a place or area, but for a language and the people who speak it. They are to be found, generally speaking, within a large triangle that reaches from the city of Madras on the south half-way across the South Indian Peninsula to the west, northwards to the borders of Orissa, and is bounded on the east by the sea-coast. This includes practically the whole of the Madras Presidency north of Madras itself and the major part of the State of Hyderabad. There are few towns of any importance and the population is almost entirely rural. The people are of Dravidian stock, closely akin to the Tamils and other racial groups of South India, which can probably be reckoned among the oldest in the country. The Telugu language, which is liquid and melodious, has sometimes been called the Italian of the East. The old Sanskrit name for the Telugu country is the Andhra Desa, and this term is frequently used in reference to their ancient culture which is rich in poetry, music and fine literature.

The new Bishop already knew the Telugu language and was at great pains to master its literary style as well as the village idiom. He loved the Andhra Desa with its fine old culture, which he did his utmost to preserve as a part of the heritage of the Telugu Church. As Assistant to Bishop Whitehead, he travelled extensively among the Telugu people and soon came to know intimately the missions already established, on the eastern side between the rivers Kistna and Godavary, by the C.M.S., and in the western area around Kurnool, Nandyal and Cuddapah, by the S.P.G. With his ready charm and courtesy, his wise and sympathetic counsel and his whole-hearted desire to promote Indian leadership, he soon won the affection and respect even of those who had been most strongly opposed to his appointment. As early as April 1913, after spending Holy Week and Easter at Nandyal, he was referred to there as " Our Bishop " and the account of his visit concluded with the words : " We felt we were taking leave of a real Father-in-God." The Dornakal fashion of referring to him and Mrs. Azariah in Telugu as " Father " and " Mother " with the honorific attached as a mark of affectionate respect, soon spread, and they became known far and wide as " Honourable Father and Mother ".

Meanwhile, Dornakal itself was growing rapidly. Land had been acquired on the other side of the railway from the old brewery where a modest two-roomed bungalow soon accommodated the Bishop, his family and his office until a house of more reasonable size could be built. The boys' school and workshops soon sprang up and the old compound was left to the girls, where they remain to this day. The little old church, very hot and rather dark, but very much loved, frequently enlarged yet never large enough, continued in use until it finally gave way to the famous Cathedral in 1939; but that was still a long way ahead, although the foundation stone was actually laid as early as 1914 and subsequently transferred to another place, Dornakal being thus probably the only Cathedral to possess the distinction of having its foundation stone laid twice over !

The Bishop's own recollections of the early days are vivid and amusing. Travelling was exceedingly slow and difficult. There were no roads in the whole of the Dornakal area (Dornakal itself cannot boast of one even yet !) and the only means of progression were by bullock-cart or on foot. To avoid the heat the Bishop usually travelled by night. The Christians in the villages through which he had to pass always met the cart to offer their welcome with drums, music and garlands. Torches would be held in his face to make sure he was awake and the ceremony was often repeated several times during the night ! Dummagudem, on the far side of the Godavary, was only reached after four nights' halt on the way. They dare not undertake the journey across the tiger-infested forest except in the company of four or five carts, and huge fires had to be kept alight around the camp at night. To-day it is possible to leave Dornakal after breakfast and arrive at Dummagudem in time for tea !

On one occasion, in the Kurnool district, the Bishop set off early in the morning to celebrate Holy Communion in a village six miles away. On arrival it was discovered that the Communion vessels had been taken to the wrong village and two stalwart young men were told to run and fetch them. Meanwhile, as the congregation had already sung themselves hoarse for nearly an hour, it was decided to start the service and the Bishop was requested to go on preaching until the young men appeared. The sermon lasted one hour and twenty minutes ! Only once was he attacked by thieves. His party was striking camp in the early morning and all was ready packed in the tents with the Bishop sleeping outside. At two in the morning he saw the luggage being carried away, as he fondly imagined by the camp servants, ready to be loaded up in the carts —only to discover shortly after that he had been robbed under his very nose ! A hue and cry ensued and at 5 a.m. the search-party of about twenty stalwart people with sticks came running in, breathless with excitement, to say they had heard the thieves breaking open the boxes about a mile away. "What did you do? " asked the Bishop. " Put out our lamps for fear they should see us and ran to tell you," was the disconcerting reply !

The shortage of clergy everywhere was very serious. In one large area the only ordained priest was the district missionary who had under him one Indian deacon. During the hot weather and the rains the deacon performed the essential ministrations until such time as the missionary could again reach the outlying villages. Thus marriages, following the immemorial custom of the Indian village, would take place at the height of the hot season and the young couples would receive the priestly blessing at a later date. But towards the end of his long career the missionary became bitten with the study of medicine and could not tear himself away from his medical books, so that when the Bishop arrived one March for a confirmation tour, the more distant villages had received no priestly ministrations for over a year. He was surprised to note, on arrival at the first place, an unusually large number of couples presenting themselves for the marriage blessing; his surprise deepened when, later in the day, the brides appeared to be churched and later still brought a collection of lusty infants to be baptized!

Another result of the shortage of clergy was that the preparation for confirmation was often stereotyped and inadequate, the candidates having carefully memorized the answers to the catechism, not expecting to be questioned on anything else. When they were seated for examination the Bishop would frequently begin in a friendly way: "What is your name? Where is your village? How far have you walked?" to be met invariably with the reply: "My godfathers and godmothers in my baptism . . . !" The village people, however, soon got used to Azariah's spirited methods of teaching and catechizing and answered with perfect freedom. One woman, on being asked what was necessary for the inward growth of her child, replied with all seriousness, "Castor oil!" These somewhat trivial instances serve to show how completely immersed the Bishop was in getting into the life of the rural community and in studying the needs and opportunities for the Church in the villages. It was this knowledge and experience, which he made so peculiarly his own, that resulted in his becoming so outstandingly "village-minded" among the Christian leaders of India.

All his time, however, was not spent in the Telugu country, for he worked in close association with Bishop Whitehead in all parts of the Madras diocese. The deep friendship between them made this partnership a very

46

happy one and Bishop Whitehead's interest in the Telugu Church never flagged. The older man's mature wisdom and prayerful patience were a great source of comfort to his young colleague in meeting and overcoming some of the hindrances, frictions and jealousies which were inseparable from his position and under which his ardent spirit frequently chafed. Their relationship ripened with every year that passed into a deeper blend of respect and love, reverence and intimacy.

Tinnivelly also claimed some of Azariah's attention and his first reception there as Bishop, in 1913, reveals the pride of the Tamil Christians in their illustrious son. The engine of his train was festooned with greenery, and at every station he was garlanded according to the Indian traditional welcome. The noise of the train rumbling over the Tinnivelly bridge was drowned by the cheers of the crowd on either side. At Palamcotta the procession, headed by two bands (probably playing different tunes !), passed under thirty triumphal arches, while guns and rockets were let off at intervals. When he left Nazareth for the home of his childhood at Megnanapuram, twelve young men insisted upon drawing his bullock-cart through miles of loose sandy soil, and the joyful enthusiasm of his own beloved village exceeded all the rest. Many people had come miles to see him and in one day alone he received over three hundred garlands. For once a prophet was not without honour in his own country !

The first great war brought its troubles and anxieties, shortage of funds, soaring prices, difficulties of communication with England and doubts about the future. But the work of the Kingdom did not slacken, and when the Metropolitan made a visitation of the Dornakal Diocese in 1917 there was cause for deep satisfaction. Church membership had almost doubled in five years, the number of ordained clergy had increased from six to twelve, and the offerings of the people were going steadily up. The evangelistic work done by the Christians themselves was noteworthy and a big summer school, presided over by Azariah, gave the Metropolitan the opportunity to testify to " the ideal relations existing between the Bishop and the workers ". A more epoch-making part of the visitation took place in other parts of the Telugu country, at Ellore by invitation of the C.M.S. missionaries, and at Nandyal at the request of the S.P.G. On both these occasions the Metropolitan and Bishop Whitehead, in conference with all the clergy, both Indian and European, were asked if all the Anglican missions in the Andhra Desa might be included in the Dornakal Diocese and thus come under the direct jurisdiction of Bishop Azariah. Surely no greater tribute could have been paid to the person and work of the first Indian Bishop than this remarkable fact, that in five short years people who had previously shown grave doubts over his appointment and even declared themselves unwilling to accept the authority of an Indian, should spontaneously request to be allowed the privilege of working in his diocese. There was no doubt about the sympathy of the two older Bishops. At their recommendation the Episcopal Synod, moving somewhat cautiously, first agreed that the terms of the Commission given to the Bishop of Dornakal by the Bishop of Madras in 1913 be extended to include a general authority to exercise episcopal functions throughout the whole of the Telugu area and, in 1920, Bishop Azariah was authorized to go forward with the organization of a Diocesan Council which would unite in one Bishopric the whole of the Anglican Church in the Andhra Desa. This was achieved and finally ratified by the Episcopal Synod in 1922.

When, therefore, Bishop Azariah went to England in 1920 to attend the Lambeth Conference he knew that he would return to administer a diocese roughly the size of England, in which the Christian adherents numbered about 90,000. As the only Indian member of the Conference, he aroused special interest and was the strong

48

protagonist of the indigenous Church. He had already taken the initiative in India in the matter of Church Union, and his plea for a more sympathetic approach to this thorny question was deeply impressive. He was received everywhere with a courtesy and kindliness that won his heart, and was honoured by Cambridge University, which conferred on him the LL.D. degree. He returned to India to take over his new responsibilities, and a year later had to say good-bye to his beloved counsellor and friend, Bishop Whitehead, whose retirement broke up a partnership which had brought untold joy and strength to Azariah and which had produced a friendship that was to continue unbroken through years of correspondence.

An address given by Bishop Azariah at Madras in 1919 on the thorny problem of the transfer of responsibility from mission to Church gives an insight into his mind at this time, and shows the lines along which he progressed steadily towards his ideal of an indigenous Church, coupled with the sober grasp of realities which was so characteristic of all his thought. Having pointed out how the political reforms were whetting the appetite of Indian Christians for independence and freedom of expression, and urged that the Church could not surely lag behind the State in these matters, he delivered his own balanced judgment. " Our young theologians want entire autonomy at one step ; sober minds will be willing to wait . . . but legitimate aspirations must be met." These he defined as follows. First, the transfer of authority to Churches, not individuals, hence the urgent need for ecclesiastical organization, as distinct from that of the mission, and the abandonment of the fallacy that the mission is the Church. Secondly, the autocracy of the district missionary, a cause of suppressed irritation to Indian Christian leaders, to be curtailed and much of their power transferred to the local Church. This would involve the training of the laity to take their rightful place in the government of their own

Church. Thirdly, Indian leaders to be sought for in all ranks of the laity and the whole Church trained towards self-support and indigenous leadership. For all this two things were vitally necessary, and for these he appealed both to the missionaries and the older generation of Indian Christians. " Believe in men, believe in the Holy Spirit. A man's belief in himself is often the result of others' belief in him. Do not be afraid to take risks. *Trust men.*" These are indeed the authentic accents of Azariah of Dornakal as the whole of his subsequent life was to prove.

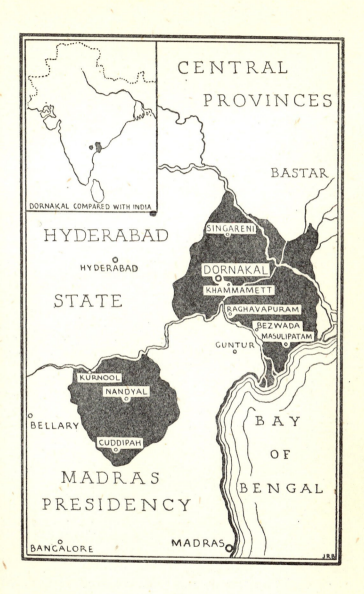

CENTRAL

PROVINCES

BASTAR

DORNAKAL COMPARED WITH INDIA

HYDERABAD

HYDERABAD

STATE

SINGARENI

DORNAKAL

KHAMMAMETT

RAGHAVAPURAM

BEZWADA

MASULIPATAM

GUNTUR

KURNOOL

NANDYAL

BELLARY

CUDDIPAH

MADRAS

PRESIDENCY

BAY

OF

BENGAL

BANGALORE

MADRAS

JRB

51

V. THE MASS MOVEMENT

Now the stage is fully set for a dynamic advance towards the building up of a Church, truly indigenous in life and worship, and for the development of a personality who will, undoubtedly, be accounted one of the greatest Christian leaders of his own or any other generation. The period is one of opportunity and expansion almost unparalleled in the history of Christendom. The setting is purely rural and in order to fill in the background it is necessary to know something of the life of village India. But this is to know the real India, that " continent of villages ", for it is estimated that nine-tenths of her teeming millions live in her 750,000 villages and get their living from the land. And, as the national life of India depends upon the well-being, or otherwise, of her rural community, so the heart of the Indian Church beats in the village congregations. Bishop Azariah became a religious leader of world-wide significance because he was primarily and devotedly a Father-in-God to his own people. He was, in fact, always first and foremost Azariah of Dornakal.

The structure of Indian rural society is based upon two deep-rooted institutions : the life of the family and the life of the village. The importance of the family as a unit cannot be over-estimated; the authority of its senior members is supreme; the claims and responsibilities of its lesser members practically nil. Marriage is a family contract, a financial arrangement, entered into by the elders of both parties and often arranged down to the last detail before the unfortunate bride or bridegroom is even informed, much less consulted. Thus all actions or decisions, small or great, must receive the sanction of the family.

Beyond the life of the family lies the life of the village

built up upon the rigid structure of caste. In a Telugu village there are roughly three main divisions. At one end of the pole are the Brahmins, a small group of the priestly caste, forming the real aristocracy and ruling class, although by no means the wealthiest section of the community. At the other end are the outcastes, untouchable, segregated in their own portion of the village in the direst poverty and degradation. Between these two extremes lies an enormous middle class, generally known as the Sudras but subdivided again and again into endless sub-castes, and embracing an infinite variety of occupations and shades of social standing, from landlords and farmers down to the humbler artisans. No outsider can ever hope to understand all the ramifications of caste, but they are known and observed, down to the last and minutest detail, by the smallest village child. Furthermore, the Telugu people have an added complication in that there are two groups among the outcastes. The Malas are weavers by tradition, although now, owing to the competition of mill-made cloth, most of the looms lie idle and the people work in the fields. The Madigas are leather-workers, an occupation which in itself renders them unclean to the caste Hindu, since they have to handle the skins of dead animals. Moreover, their dire poverty has frequently reduced them to the level of eating carrion. To the caste people, both Mala and Madiga are equally untouchable; between themselves there is a great gulf fixed, which has issued in a hereditary feud that hinders them from making common cause even out of their common misery. Thus, a casual walk through the veritable rabbit-warren of any Telugu village reveals the existence of these innumerable communal groups. Brahmin houses cluster round the Temple; landlords blossom out into double-story buildings with richly carved doorways and flamboyant decorations; shepherds, potters, carpenters, goldsmiths and so forth, each occupy their own little bit of the village. Finally, beyond a rigid dividing line, are the miserable hovels of Mala and Madiga, with broken-down walls and gaping roofs amid stagnant pools and piles of refuse. Even in the generally low standard of cleanliness and order that prevails in an Indian village the squalor of the outcaste hamlet has to be seen to be believed.

This systematized form of living has had some very important results on the life and mentality of village India. Obviously, it has created divisions such as even the most ardent Hindu reformer has so far found unbridgeable. When, by every rule of society, people may neither intermarry nor even inter-dine outside their own little sub-caste, there is little hope for united thought or action. Yet, paradoxically, caste has also produced the most elaborate system of economic co-operation. For the farmer owns the land, employs all the villagers as his labourers and pays them, at harvest time, with the grain upon which they live for the rest of the year. In return, the potter makes the pots, the carpenter the ploughs and the blacksmith the farm implements, for their common landlord, while the weaver weaves the clothes, the dhobi washes them and the goldsmith fashions the jewels for the great man's household. The same system of barter and exchange holds good throughout the village and, since their needs are few and simple, every village has been, until recently, a little self-contained and self-supporting republic. Inevitably, this has induced a mentality which thinks always in terms of the community rather than the individual. If, in your walks abroad in the country lanes, you meet with the friendly village people and ask them who they are, the reply will always be given in the plural thus : " We are farmers, they are shepherds, those are weavers," as the case may be. And this is hardly surprising when you realize that, from the cradle to the grave, they live, move and have their being as ciphers in the complicated social system which constitutes the only world they know. Finally, and most tragically, the caste system has produced the outcastes, some eighty million people, condemned, simply by the accident of their birth, to be regarded by the vast majority of their fellow-countrymen as untouchable, living in a state of poverty, dirt and degradation such as beggars description, a state of affairs in which, for the most part, the great Hindu community has calmly acquiesced for over a thousand years. To quote the late Mr. G. K. Ghokale, one of India's ablest statesmen during the last century : " We may touch a cat, we may touch a dog, we may touch any other animal, but the touch of these human beings is pollution ! And so complete is now the mental degradation of these people that they themselves see nothing in this treatment to resent, and acquiesce in it as though nothing better were their due."

Into this elaborate structure of communal life Christianity has come by means of the mass movement. That is to say, during the past eighty odd years enormous numbers of people, chiefly from among the outcastes, have been received into the Church, not singly, nor only in families, but in large groups varying in size from about fifty to two hundred. There are many sincere Christians who have doubted the wisdom of thus admitting into the Christian communion large numbers drawn from the lowest strata of society, the purity of whose motives has often been called in question; but Bishop Azariah always opposed this point of view most strenuously. As we have already seen, he was above all things village-minded, knowing every turn of village life and loving most dearly the village people, and he it is, more than anyone else, who has helped the Indian Church to see these mass movements as the logical outcome of the communal life of the village. Where people are accustomed to think always in terms of their community and to live out their lives as members of a group, it is both natural and inevitable that they should move towards Christianity along the same lines. Admittedly their motives in the first place may be mixed. There is the herd instinct bidding them follow friends and relations. There is the desire for self-improvement, education, and above all salvation from the general degradation of their lot. When they give as their reason : " Because we are bad and want to be better ", they are expressing a deep-rooted human longing. But Bishop Azariah was wont to point out that the motives which drove the Prodigal Son home were neither very pure nor very lofty, and he urged that it was the task of the Church to accept the opportunity thus offered and lead these seekers after a better life to find it in Christ and desire Him for Himself alone.

While the growth of the Church in numbers has been phenomenal, what is even more striking is the transformation wrought by the power of the Holy Spirit. It is easy to understand how the Gospel which tells of the Fatherhood of God and the brotherhood of man, the equal value of every individual in the heart of the Creator, should be hailed as the veritable Good News of salvation to men and women condemned by their fellow-men to the depths of untouchability. But St. Paul has shown us only too clearly that, in any generation, the liberating power of the Gospel may prove a heady wine to people born and bred in slavery. In this respect there are many points of similarity between the early Church in the Roman Empire and the Christian community in India. In both cases " not many wise after the flesh, not many mighty, not many noble " are called, but there is the same liberation of mind and spirit after centuries of oppression and degradation. It takes a man of genius, both temporal and spiritual, to accept courageously these great outpourings of the Spirit and guide them into enduring channels, and God has perhaps shown His most signal mercy to the Church of India, at this most critical period of her history, by raising up a leader of such indomitable courage, such breadth of vision and such great spiritual stature as Bishop Azariah.

Instances of the transformation which has come about in the villages through the Christian religion are not far to seek; they may be found, with few exceptions, wherever there is a Christian congregation. Cleanliness in place of squalor, temperance instead of drunkenness, a concerted effort towards clean-living, honest dealing and truthfulness, above all the discovery of that most precious of human possessions, self-respect; all these are the outward and visible signs of an inward and spiritual transfiguration. It might have been expected that it would take many generations of teaching and experience of the Christian way of life to lift the untouchables up to the cultural level even of the rest of the village, but in point of fact it is most of all in the rural Churches, among the outcaste community, that the evidence of the Christian dynamic is unmistakable. Moreover, the evidence for this comes from many sources that are quite unbiased. For instance, it was an official of the Indian Civil Service who wrote in his census report : " The missionaries have all these years been providing the *corpus sanum* (if one thing is noticeable about Indian Christians it is their greater cleanliness in dress and habits), and now comes the appearance of the *mens sana*. The children of the first generation of Christian converts are now growing up . . . and their generation is beginning to make itself felt. The Hindu fellow-members of their former community have now to acknowledge, not only that the Christians are better off, but also that they are better men." More striking still was the testimony continually offered to the Bishop by the caste people of the villages and stored up by him as a treasured memorial to his beloved Mala and Madiga Christians, in whom he had such confidence. Who could have a better chance of judging than the village magistrates ? One of these on being asked how he found the Christians in his district replied :

" Formerly every decent man shunned their hamlet after sunset, the drinking, quarrelling and foul language were too loathsome for words, and cattle poisoning (for the sake of their skins) was common. Now it is unknown in Christian villages and the music of lyrics and songs from the village chapel fills the evening air."

Another, pointing to the Christians, said : " Their fathers and grandfathers lived by plunder, nothing was safe in the village. Now we can leave our doors open and sleep in peace. It is a good religion."

On one occasion two high-caste Hindus stood for a whole hour in absolute silence watching a confirmation service, and when the Bishop came out said to him reflectively :

" We know these people well; they are our servants, and their fathers and forefathers served our fathers and forefathers. They are inferior to us in caste, wealth, education and looks; yet as we looked at their faces we could not fail to see that they had got something which we have not got."

Most striking of all were the villages in which the caste people mended their ways to match the outcaste Christians. " We are ashamed of many things when we see the outcastes living as these Christians do." Such testimonials could never be forgotten.

All this does not imply that every congregation was perfect, every Christian a paragon. The Bishop himself gives the following instance to the contrary. " Six men of caste came to me and asked for baptism. They had been watching the outcastes in a certain village church and had seen that since becoming Christians they had been getting ahead of the caste people. ' They will be better than we are if we do not become Christians,' they said. That very day the pastor of that village church had complained to me of the sins of that very congregation. So I said that these church members were not perfect, to which the caste men replied : ' Yes, there are black sheep in every flock, but we know what they were ten years ago and what they are now.' "

Other instances of the uprush of cultural power released by the Holy Spirit are to be found in the outburst of song and drama which has swept over all sections of the Christian Church in the Telugu country during the past forty years or more. Christian lyrics set to Telugu tunes are a feature of Christian worship; the Gospel story, sung in ballad form, may be heard in the fields in harvest time; the old village dances, redeemed from their heathen associations, are immensely popular at Christian festivals; musical dramas, based on the stories of Biblical heroes, draw huge crowds wherever they are presented. The Church has once again come into its own as the guardian and inspiration of all that is good and true and beautiful in the ancient heritage of the Indian village, and no one rejoiced in this development more whole-heartedly, or fostered it more enthusiastically, than Bishop Azariah. The Indian music has always been a feature of Dornakal Cathedral. The Bishop himself usually selected, with infinite care, the music required for any special service in which he took part. He encouraged the writers of Scriptural drama, proposing new subjects, sitting wide-awake through the lengthiest performances and then pro-ducing suggestions or criticisms, appreciative, helpful, or devastating, as the occasion demanded, but always stimulating to further and better efforts. He specially loved the rich anthology of Telugu lyrics on the Passion of our Lord and usually started the Three Hours' Service on Good Friday with a prolonged period of quiet devo-tional singing of some of these exquisite meditations on the sufferings and death of Christ. It may perhaps be remarked in passing that, whereas, in the West, the joyous festivals of Christmas and Easter have produced some of our best-loved hymns, while the events of Passion-tide seem to have been singularly unproductive, in the East it appears to be exactly the reverse. At all events the Telugu genius has certainly not risen to the same heights for its Easter Alleluias as it has in its devotion to the Crucified Lord.

The Christian life in the villages is thus the setting against which we have to see the life and work of Bishop Azariah, for his name has become so intimately associated with the mass movement that people have sometimes talked as if he originated it. This is, of course, a gross exaggeration. He entered into a great heritage of opportunity at a time when India was ripe for a deep stirring of the Spirit and, to some extent, reaped where other men had sown. His unique contribution to the evangelization of India lay not so much in what he did himself as in how he inspired others to act, and the tremendously increased pace of the movement which, in barely a quarter of a century, brought the Telugu Anglican Communion from 90,000 to nearly a quarter of a million, was certainly, under God, the result of methods initiated by Azariah. The truth is that the irresistible momentum which carried all before it, gathering speed as it went, came from the Christians themselves and can be explained by one word, Witness. Now, here we touch the very core of Azariah's influence and teaching, for it seemed to him that the responsibility for spreading Christ's Kingdom on earth should rest chiefly upon ordinary Christian men and women, each giving his witness by word and deed, through the evidence of a transformed life and an active part in evangelism. His own words describe how he acted upon this conviction.

" In the Acts, the Christ seems to go into the background; it is the brethren, the disciples, the Church that take the place of Christ. . . . *The Church continued where Christ left off.* . . . Every member of the Church is expected to go forward in the army of those continuing what Christ came to do . . . otherwise he denies his baptism.

" ' Every Christian a witness ' is a slogan of our efforts at evangelism in India. We have been getting little groups of baptized persons together and training them to go about and answer the simple questions of the Indian villagers. One was asked : ' Have you seen God ? ', and his answer was : ' Sirs, you knew me two years ago. I was a drunkard. You know me now. I do not think I should have had all this change if I had not seen Jesus Christ.' There is no better answer and no better way of witnessing for God.

" In the early Church it was the common man who spread the Gospel of Christ . . . from slave to slave, from soldier to soldier, from artisan to artisan. . . . The sharing of experience with others adds to our own Christian experience. Let some men just stand somewhere as Christians ; let them face a non-Christian crowd ; let some-one else do the preaching and the singing ; the experience of just standing for Christ will drive them to their knees before Christ. . . .

" I used to go around among the churches and have the baptized members place their hands on their heads (as if in the act of baptism) and repeat after me : ' I am a baptized Christian. Woe unto me if I preach not the Gospel.' Many people ask others : ' Are you saved ? ' It were better if they asked : ' Are you *saving* ? ' "

In this speech, made to the Tambaram Conference towards the end of his life, Azariah reveals the secret which underlay that mighty movement in the Telugu villages. It was a contagion which spread from man to man, from group to group, from village to village. There was no question of ' counting heads ', or glorifying in numbers. The Church Councils, ever put to it to find funds from their desperately strained resources, might well have put the brake on had it been possible. But the growing stream, fed by fresh rivulets from village after village, had become a mighty river ; innumerable sparks, lighted in the hearts of the simplest village Christians, had become a great fire. Azariah had indeed lived to see the day when the evangelization of India had far out-stripped the power and personal influence of the foreign missionary.

61

And so, led by a man whose vision was rooted in an unquenchable faith in the Holy Spirit and in men, the Christian Church takes its place in the life of the Indian village, not as just one more community in the complicated communal system already there, but as the Holy Community in which alone mankind can be redeemed from the forces of evil, liberated by the power of the Spirit, and learn to dedicate all life to the service of the One, True God. " Witnesses to the Resurrection " was the name proudly claimed by the Apostles as they went forth to turn the world upside-down; this same witness to the power of the Risen Christ to revolutionize the lot of the outcaste is being proclaimed once again all over the Telugu country. The Gospel of Salvation must issue in the foundation of the Holy Community, but as soon as the Church is anywhere established it must itself become the instrument for evangelization. Moreover, unless the witness of a redeemed life and the ministry of the word go hand in hand, either will prove unavailing. The Telugu Church has shown once again, beyond all possibility of denial, that the glory of the Resurrection is irresistible and the power of the Holy Spirit invincible because, now as in the first century, no man can fail to take notice of Christians who have really been with Jesus.

We have now seen how the Indian villages formed the setting in which Bishop Azariah's greatest work was done. The rural community with its deep-rooted social customs; the outcastes in their extreme poverty and degradation; the mass movement spreading like a heath fire from village to village; the Church emerging as the Holy Community, possessed of supernatural, transforming power— these are the strands that formed the pattern of which he, under God, was called to be the master weaver. However far his influence eventually extended among Christian leaders, however great his vision for the Kingdom of God on earth, that vision first flowered among the congregations of his beloved Telugu villages and his influence was largely due to the abundant and evident fruits of his labours. That he had entered into other men's labours, reaping the fruits of their sowing as well as his own, he would have been the first to acknowledge, and, in order fully to appreciate the measure of his stature as a Diocesan Bishop, it is necessary to understand something of this heritage into which he entered when the full charge of the Anglican Church in the Telugu country descended upon him.

One of the striking things in the history of the evangelization of India is the noteworthy part played by British Government officials, often God-fearing laymen whose great desire was to alleviate the miserable condition of the outcastes through the love of Christ, and whose appeals to the missionary societies of Great Britain frequently called forth the pioneer missionaries. In these days, when debunking the British Empire has become a popular pastime, perhaps it is as well that this fact should be placed to the credit side of the British administration in India! There are two such men who may be justly regarded as the founders of Christian Missions in the Telugu country. The first of these, in point of time, was an Anglo-Indian civil servant, William Howell, who was stationed in the early part of the nineteenth century at Cuddapah, then a prosperous town in the south-west corner of the Telugu area. His charm of manner quickly endeared him to all whom he met. Being deeply religious, he greatly desired to see the Church established in the region where he worked, and spent his leisure, as he went about, preaching to all who would listen to him. So strongly did the claim of the Telugu people appeal to him that, when still quite a young man, he began to contemplate resigning his Government post and giving his whole time to evangelism. The only Christian work within reach at that time was being carried on by the London Missionary Society, and in 1822 Howell was appointed as their resident missionary in Cuddapah, although he was by tradition an Anglican.

The Christian congregation in Cuddapah grew steadily, but their life was not without its excitements. In 1832 they were the centre of a vicious riot engineered by the Cuddapah Pathans,[1] who were notoriously fanatical and who decided to avenge their grievances against the British Government on the poor little Christian congregation. In the hot days of June, just before the monsoon, when tempers are often strained to breaking-point, the Pathans threw the bleeding body of a dead rat into the Mohammedan mosque on the eve of a feast day and spread the rumour that it was the corpse of a pig placed there by the Christians! A terrible riot ensued. The Moslems, in a fury, surged towards the Christian quarter and the Christians fled for their lives to Howell's bungalow, pursued by the crowd. The situation was saved by the superb

[1] A north Indian race of fanatical Hindus who frequently penetrate to the south as money-lenders.

courage of the Sub-Collector, Charles Edward Macdonald, a Scotsman worthy of the name he bore. In answer to Howell's urgent appeal for help, Macdonald went in person, accompanied only by a few soldiers of the treasury guard. He was torn in pieces by the mob and the guard shared his fate, but the crowd, seeing what they had done, were suddenly sobered and dissolved in panic, leaving the street empty save for the dead bodies of Macdonald and his faithful guard. The Christians were saved and the Church lived on. By 1842 they were one hundred strong and, in that year, William Howell decided to seek episcopal orders. He was accepted as a missionary of the S.P.G. and half his flock went with him. He can therefore be reckoned as the father of both the Anglican and Congregational Churches on the western side of the Telugu country.

On the eastern side a more highly placed Government official and equally faithful servant of God filled a similar role. This was John Goldingham, who came to Masulipatam as Collector of the Kistna District in 1836. He dearly loved the Telugu people, of whom he wrote : " They are naturally one of the most interesting and hopeful of Indian peoples, possessing a great manliness of character and independence and strong natural affections." As a good churchman, it grieved him " that no clergyman of the Church of England has ever been known to preach to these ten millions of people ", and he set himself to work and pray for the establishment of the Church among the Telugus. In those days Masulipatam was a flourishing little sea-port with a large and prosperous European population, and Goldingham soon gathered round him a group of like-minded friends, enthused the local residents, collected money, and appealed persistently to the missionary societies of England, until, finally, the C.M.S. agreed to take them under its wing. The first missionaries set sail from England in the spring of 1841, but by the time they reached India, five months later, Goldingham had been transferred to Guntur. At first he and Robert Noble, the great pioneer missionary of the C.M.S., laid plans to evangelize both the Kistna and Guntur districts, but this proved too much for their slender resources, and when, shortly after, the Evangelical Lutheran Church of America offered to establish a mission at Guntur, Goldingham gladly fell in with the suggestion and welcomed them heartily. He thus became, like William Howell in the west, the founder of the two oldest Churches on the eastern side.

This parallel between the missions established on the two sides of the Dornakal Diocese continued in the most striking manner. Howell was in the habit of paying frequent visits to the jail at Cuddapah and there he came in contact with a man belonging to the Mala community called Akutu Nancharu, a seller of thread, who for some crime not recorded served a lengthy term of imprisonment. On his release, he sought out Mr. Howell and begged him to come and preach in his village some fifty miles away. The challenge was taken up by two brothers, Telugu Christians called Alfred and Basil Wood, who followed Nancharu to his home. There, amid the innumerable villages of the rich fertile plain bounded by the harsh, rocky Red Hills on the west, and the dim, mysterious, forest-clad range of the Black Hills to the east, the Christian religion took root among the outcastes of Mala origin. The first baptism took place in 1852 and others followed rapidly. Six years later the formidable barrier of the Black Hills, with its wild animals and equally dreaded forest tribe, was crossed and the work continued on the other side.

By 1870 forty congregations had been established with close upon 1,700 baptized Christians and well over 1,000 more being instructed. But their lot was by no means a bed of roses. When these outcaste Christians used their new-found freedom to repudiate the village gods and withheld themselves from the ancient sacrifices, the caste people scented danger at the very heart of their citadel. The Christians were refused work, beaten, had their houses burned over their heads and false charges put upon them in the courts, but nothing could quench the Spirit. Then came a truly searching test. In 1876-77 the rains failed. Day after day men gazed longingly at the clouds which would not break. Night after night the drums throbbed through the darkness summoning them to sacrifice. The famine which followed was one of the worst and the death-rate appalling. On the heels of the famine came cholera, until almost the only sound to be heard in the villages was the wailing of the living over the dead. The Hindus did not hesitate to accuse the Christians of calling down the wrath of the gods upon their defenceless heads and bitter was their animosity. Some of the Christians went back; it could hardly be otherwise at that stage. When the worst was over, with whole villages completely ruined, congregations decimated by disease and starvation, chapels and schools lying in utter disrepair, it must have seemed as if the young Church had received a blow from which it would not recover. But in the Kingdom of God there is no retreat. With courage and faith purged through this ordeal the Church still went forward, gathering momentum every year, until by the end of the century there were 10,000 Christians and twenty years later the number was nearly doubled. Churches were built, schools and hospitals arose and flourished as the mass movement gradually spread through the villages and the foundations of the Holy Community were well and truly laid.

To return to the eastern side of the Telugu country. In 1842 the C.M.S. missionaries started work in Masulipatam and, in 1843, a school was opened for high-caste boys. The results were disappointing, for seven years later the boys were still boasting that there would never be a convert to the Christian religion in Masulipatam and when, in 1852, two baptisms did actually take place, they had to be performed at dead of night for fear of a riot. The real mass movement did not begin until 1859 and centred round the romantic figure of Pagollu Venkayya, a man who had a certain affinity with Nancharu of the Cuddapah district in that he, too, was well known to the police! Venkayya, also a Mala of outcaste origin, was a man of great force of character, given to highway robbery on an extensive scale, who had long been a local legend for his daring exploits and his ingenuity in escaping from prison. But in middle life a deep inner desire for God, made stronger by the loss of a dearly loved child, drove him forth on a spiritual search, for what he did not clearly know, and brought him to Bezwada, then a poky little town on the banks of the river Kistna, attractive only to pilgrims who came to bathe in its sacred waters. Here, at the time of a festival, when the sandy bed of the river was thronged with devotees of the Hindu religion, a chance conversation with an Indian Guru sent Venkayya climbing the steep hill leading to the mission bungalow, then occupied by a certain Mr. Darling. This good man had reached the lowest ebb of discouragement. His efforts to evangelize the Telugus had resulted apparently in complete failure and, on this hot April afternoon, behind the closed shutters of his house, he was pouring out the bitterness of his soul to God, little knowing that one of the great romances of the Gospel was about to involve him. Venkayya's arrival, during the sacred period of the afternoon siesta, brought Mr. Darling's Hindu butler out in a rage, the noise of which roused the missionary from his devotions and brought him face to face with Venkayya. Through the long, hot afternoon Mr. Darling preached the Gospel and Venkayya listened until, in the evening, he stood up and said simply : " This is my God and my Saviour. Long have I sought Him, now I will serve Him." Like Nancharu he thought at once of his own village and persuaded the somewhat unwilling Mr. Darling to undertake the journey out there in the hottest month of the year—for which he was amply repaid by results. By the complete repudiation of his former manner of life Venkayya was able to give a personal witness to the power of the Holy Spirit that proved irresistible. From village after village people flocked to listen and stayed to learn. Once more the mass movement had begun among the outcastes and Venkayya alone brought over 700 people to the feet of Christ.

Yet, once again, there was to be a tragic ordeal for the Christian community. By 1864 the Church seemed well and truly established. There were thousands of Christians among the outcastes of the villages; a sprinkling of caste Hindus in the towns had also been baptized and of these the two who were first baptized by night had also been ordained. Then came a fearful catastrophe. A cyclone, accompanied by a tidal wave, engulfed Masulipatam, sweeping away the port and ravaging the whole countryside. It was a night of terror in the little town when, as far as the eye could see, there were only the surging waves of the dark waters, capped with phosphorescence and whipped to a seething fury by the gale. Houses were swept away and hundreds of people lost their lives. The English community fled and the town never regained its prosperity. Even now people still shudder in their beds if a gale gets up in the late monsoon. Thus, once again, the very existence of the young Church was threatened by a staggering loss of life and property; but, as before, with steadfast courage and loyalty, it weathered the storm and continued to grow apace. Masulipatam, true to its early traditions, became a great centre of Christian education, while Bezwada, where roads, canals and railways gradually converged, became more and more the centre of the Telugu country and of the life of the Church in the Kistna District.

We can now see something of the task which faced Bishop Azariah when, in 1920, these two great areas, each with its own sphere of missionary work, were added to

the Diocese of Dornakal. In the west was the Church
which had sprung up on either side of the Black Hills and
now extended over the Red Hills to the borders of the
Hyderabad State at Kurnool. In the east was the Church
of the Kistna District, spreading northward to the other
great river, Godavary, and westward up the line of the
Nizam's railway till it touched the existing Diocese of
Dornakal in the region of Khammamett. Geographically,
these two great Christian communities did not even adjoin
one another, since a large belt of country occupied by the
Lutheran Church lies in between them. Together they
comprised over 70,000 souls, nearly five times the number
contained in the Diocese up to date, in a Church that had
been established for close upon eighty years, while the
Church at Dornakal itself was not yet fifteen years old.
Moreover, Dornakal had all its roots in India, and was
accustomed to think in terms of the indigenous Church,
whereas these new areas had been largely financed from
England, had had their policy shaped for them by the
British missionaries, looked for guidance and support to
two different missionary societies, representing different
traditions of churchmanship and a wider divergence of
opinion and teaching than is probably the case to-day.
It was by no means uncommon to hear the Indians talk
of themselves as S.P.G. or C.M.S. Christians! The
Bishop was therefore faced with the stupendous task of
integrating all these diverse elements into one diocese,
and all the Christians within the diocese into one family,
in such a way as to create a strong indigenous Church,
truly Catholic in faith, truly evangelical in spirit, and
wholly Indian in its outward expression.

We know how strongly Azariah felt about the thorny
question of self-government within the Church. At Edinburgh in 1910 he had summed up his convictions thus :
" There can never be real progress until the aspirations
of mature Christians to self-government and independence
are accepted, encouraged and acted upon. . . . I am fully

aware that all advance in responsibility should be made *gradually* . . . but, none the less, steadily it *should be done*. We shall only learn to walk by walking, perchance by falling and learning by our mistakes, but never by being kept in leading strings until we arrive at maturity." Two years later one of the missionaries in the Telugu country wrote : " Only when an Indian is appointed to the sole charge of a district will there be true self-govern- ment." Since that time machinery had been introduced by the Episcopal Synod designed to give Indians a full share in the Councils of their Church, and the two Bishops of Madras and Dornakal had worked out their plans to- gether, the Englishman showing his wonted sympathy with Indian aspirations, and the Indian his intimate knowledge of Indian limitations. It then remained to set the machinery in motion, and where Azariah showed a wisdom and courage ahead of his time was in his readiness to give a large measure of self-government to a Church as yet only on the threshold of adolescence, much less come to maturity, while at the same time guarding it with a strong and stern discipline. He was, in fact, prepared to trust men to the leading of the Holy Spirit, provided he could at the same time guard them from the snares of the devil.

His first step was to abolish the post of district mission- ary and hand over local authority to the Indian clergy. Villages grouped into pastorates, pastorates into dean- eries, and deaneries under Church councils provided a framework in which truly representative government by clergy and laity could gradually be developed. The super- vision of village schools and teachers, the development of strong congregational life, the forward work of evangel- ism thus passed entirely into the hands of Indians, while the relationship of paymaster and servant, as between the missionaries and the Indian workers (so severely castigated by the Bishop himself in that same Edinburgh speech), was abolished for ever. Senior Indian clergymen of proved wisdom and ability were given special responsibilities in local administration, but every pastor knew that he and he alone was responsible direct to the Bishop for the spiritual welfare of his charge. All this is, of course, a commonplace in the Church of India to-day, but twenty-five years ago, in a Church that was still in its first generation and growing rapidly, it was a step that only a man with supreme faith in God and his fellow-men would have dared to take.

It speaks volumes for Azariah's persuasive tact and the confidence he inspired that this far-reaching change should have come about in perfect harmony both with the missionaries and their societies. The Bishop of Worcester (Dr. Wilson Cash), for many years secretary of the C.M.S., has paid the Bishop this tribute : " He asked the Societies to trust him, as Bishop, to carry out a diocesan policy unifying all their work. . . . They met this generous-hearted man in a truly generous way, and he was able to lay the foundations of a true unity within the Diocese for the building up of a truly indigenous Church." What was true of the Societies was equally true of the missionaries. These men who had enjoyed such a large measure of independence and wielded such tremendous authority in their own districts were second to none in their admiration for the Bishop and loyalty in carrying out their own dethronement. Many among the younger generation became his lifelong friends and fellow-workers. The whole-hearted co-operation of such men as Ernest Tanner and Anthony Elliott of the C.M.S. and Percy Emmet and Frederick Gledstane of the S.P.G. (to mention only a few) was no small factor in the development of the Telugu Church, and the Bishop's regard for them and their work was abundantly shown when, in later years, he chose from their ranks his Assistant Bishop and several of his Archdeacons.

Ten years later, in a charge delivered to the clergy of the Diocese, the Bishop reviewed the results of his far-seeing and courageous statesmanship. Having shown the rise in the Christian community from 86,000 in 1920 to nearly 158,000 in 1930, he went on to say : " One human factor that has contributed in no small measure to this advance is the part the Indian clergy have played in the leadership of the work of this decade. . . . To-day there are twenty-five Deanery Chairmen (i.e., senior Indian clergymen administering several pastorates), some of whom have in their deaneries over 10,000 Christian people and 100 or 150 teachers of rural schools. . . . They have not proved uniformly perfect or efficient, but, without any fear of contradiction, I may assert that the Church has had in the Chairmen a body of men who have proved worthy of trust and confidence, able to carry a great weight of responsibility . . . men of marked ability and devotion, to be associated with whom has been an un-qualified joy. The policy of delegating to the Indian clergy powers and responsibilities once solely in the hands of the European missionaries has fully justified itself by its results, and no one rejoices more in these results than the missionaries themselves." And these words, spoken from full inside knowledge, were amply supported by the out-side testimony of Dr. Cash when he visited Dornakal some years later. " When I met the clergy I was immensely impressed by their virility and spiritual quality. Their parishes were the size of archdeaconries in England, and they had under them all the village teachers and evangel-ists. The Bishop placed in the forefront of his plans for the Diocese the spiritual life and message of his clergy, and I shall always remember the thoroughness with which this was carried out."

It is obvious that such a policy requires an ever-in-creasing supply of trained Indian clergy and in this, at first, the Diocese was sadly deficient. Training for the sacred ministry was therefore a most pressing need, and it became the Bishop's chief care and joy until the day of his death. He had from the beginning a distinct and unique vision and he worked towards it patiently and hopefully. First, in view of the extensive responsibilities to be vested in them, the candidates for ordination must be men who had already proved themselves able and devoted sons of the Church, faithful in life and worship, wise and understanding in their dealings with men. For the time being, if necessary, educational standards must be waived in favour of spiritual experience and personal ability, although the ultimate aim of a highly educated, trained and qualified ministry was never for a moment obscured. In the early years, as the Bishop went about the Diocese, he would sometimes call out exceptional men from their work in school or college to give their lives to the priesthood, often at great sacrifice to themselves, and some of the greatest leaders of the Telugu Church have been among those who answered this call. Secondly, Azariah was convinced that for such men a ' college ' atmosphere would not be the most helpful and he conceived the idea of a Divinity School in which the ordinands, together with their wives and families, might enrich their spiritual experience and enlarge their knowledge of the Church against the simple, homely background of family and parochial life. Thus the living quarters were to consist of a series of cottages, built round three sides of a quadrangle, in the simplest possible style, while the ' Quad ', usually envisaged as a sedate resort for dons and scholars, would serve as a playground for the children and resound with shrieks of mirth, or squalls of tribulation ! The Bishop himself would supervise the studies of the men, which would be entirely in the vernacular; their wives would attend classes taken by Mrs. Azariah; the atmosphere of Dornakal, with its whole emphasis on Church rather than Mission, would soak into their bones, and men gathered from all over this vast Diocese would grow together in the bonds of a real fellowship.

There was a long way to go, however, before this ideal

could be fully realized. The first class which came to Dornakal in 1919 was housed in temporary quarters so humble that they have to be seen to be believed ! But it contained men who were to leave their mark on the Telugu Church, and all who joined it in those memorable days declare that the happy intimacy they enjoyed with the Bishop and his wife in work and recreation and the daily inspiration of their teaching and example, more than compensated for material discomforts. Gradually, as money became available, the new living quarters went up, but eight years later the students were still using a lecture room barely ten feet square. Then, during a visit to England in 1927, the Bishop preached one Sunday morning in Salisbury Cathedral on his vision for the Indian ministry. At lunch-time he received a note containing a cheque for £1,000 to complete the Divinity School and, in course of time, the Fletcher Hall, called after the generous donor, occupied the fourth side of the quadrangle, with lecture rooms and library below and a large upper room that, for many years, served as a chapel, its wide open doors and windows affording a glorious view of the surrounding hills.

Thus there came into being an institution which has been the very heart and soul of the Dornakal Diocese. Never, however tired or busy he might be, did the Bishop miss his daily class with the ordinands, whenever he was in Dornakal. Day after day, at the hottest hour, for over twenty years, Mrs. Azariah might be seen going off to take her class for the women. The husbands played up nobly by exchanging the fountain pen for the baby while their wives were in class, and the Pastors' wives have come to have a clearly recognized status and sphere of work among the women. The Azariah of old, true to his early tradition, became a teacher of the Bible probably unsurpassed anywhere in India. He read incessantly, remembered everything he read and kept abreast of all that modern scholarship and research could contribute

75

towards Biblical knowledge. His vivid imagination, backed by his extensive study and together with his sense of humour, made both Old and New Testaments live in a way that was a revelation to most of his listeners. The patriarchs were illuminated by all the recent excavations in Bible lands; the Prophets came alive as well-known characters against a historical background extraordinarily like our own; the Book of Job was revealed as a deeply moving drama, repeating itself in every age, and the Psalms became the songs of a living, worshipping, persecuted Church. But it was perhaps most of all in his deep love and understanding of St. Paul and his genius in applying the conditions and problems, the strength and weakness, of the Church in the first century to the Telugu Church of to-day, that he rose to his greatest heights. For here we have the whole core and centre of his training of the ministry. "Teach, teach, teach," he said to his clergy. "What shall we teach? I would urge upon you all to give definite teaching on the Church and its place in the Divine Order. . . . I would emphasize our obligation to preach to our people, with no uncertain voice, the privilege of Church membership, the obligation to be loyal to its spiritual authority, the danger of breaking up its fellowship . . . and the sinfulness of any action that is likely to destroy its unity, its saintliness, its catholicity." Here surely is the authentic voice of the true Father-in-God, the man whose own vision of the One, True, Holy Catholic Church was becoming steadily and immeasurably enriched by his close contact with other Christian bodies in promoting the unity of Christendom, and who yet never failed to find the application of his vision to the humblest needs of the poorest congregation in the Telugu villages.

W E can now see how the main strands of Azariah's life and work met and found their fulfilment in his vocation as Bishop of Dornakal. India, the Gospel, the Church; the Indian Christian leader, the Evangelist, the Father-in-God; these three were all along inextricably interwoven and how he found strength for the immense activity of those strenuous years is one of the miracles of God. For he was everywhere, continually touring his huge diocese, constantly travelling the length and breadth of India, frequently voyaging abroad. In 1920 he went to England for his first Lambeth Conference. In 1923 he visited Australia and New Zealand; in 1927 England, for the third time, and Lausanne. In 1930 he was in England again for his second Lambeth Conference, this time accompanied by his wife and eldest daughter, with whom he re-visited Palestine and his favourite haunts on the Continent and also witnessed the Passion Play at Oberammergau, which left an indelible impression on his mind. In 1936 he was in Australia again, and in 1937 he paid his last visit to England for two World Conferences and the Coronation. From there he went on to the United States, where he was accorded a great reception by the Episcopal Church of America, which had already two missionaries working in the Diocese of Dornakal, and which he hoped would accept full responsibility for the area in which they were working. The Bishop felt it to be a great source of enrichment to have serving in his Diocese men and women from different countries and branches of the Anglican Communion, and welcomed whole-heartedly missionaries from Britain, Australia, New Zealand and America as well as Indians sent by the Church in Tinnivelly, Travancore and Ceylon.

On all these tours he was, of course, greatly sought after as a preacher and speaker, but what he valued most were the personal contacts he made with individuals in many parts of the world. He set tremendous store by the help which came to Dornakal through their thought and prayers, and returned from his trips abroad enriched and invigorated by giving and receiving and full of the new impressions he had gained. How he enjoyed commenting on us and criticizing our ways! One thing he envied was the village church in England, seeing in it the rich heritage of simple devotion handed down from our Christian forbears. He often said it was impossible to set foot in England without knowing it was a Christian country, yet he had few illusions regarding the decline of religion among our people and more than once, when the problems of second generation Christians in India were under discussion, he turned to the missionaries present with an apologetic twinkle and remarked : " You see, with all due deference, I don't want the Telugu Church to become like the Church of England ! " So great were the demands made upon him wherever he went and so generously were they met that it is small wonder that on his return from England in 1930 he had a breakdown in health and was forced to take a prolonged rest. After six months he returned to his labours with a zest of spirit and mental alertness that concealed any deficiency of physical strength. All his life he was a prodigious writer in English, Tamil and Telugu, and, as we have already said, an indefatigable reader, keeping abreast of current thought and events in all Church matters, while the time devoted to prayer and solid Bible study each day never slackened. Added to all else this gives some idea of the immense activity which filled every minute of his waking hours, from long before dawn until well on into the night. For years he was ably assisted by his eldest daughter,

Mercy Azariah, acting as his secretary, and the depth of understanding between them was one of the chief joys of Azariah's life.

Undoubtedly one of his greatest gifts as a bishop was his genius for entering heart and soul into every interest of the Diocese, great or small. At times he was criticized for exercising too much authority over every detail of administration and accused of having an episcopal finger in every pie. If there were any truth in this it was largely due to his vital interest in every aspect of Christian life and witness and every detail in the growth of the Church's work, from the spiritual oversight of souls to such practical items as boarding-school diet and sanitary arrangements! Those who have served, however humbly, in the golden age of this great diocese will witness to the stimulus of the Bishop's interest in the smallest of their doings, his quick grasp of every situation and the drive with which he was wont to initiate new ideas. At the same time he knew how to wait if he thought the time not yet ripe for some new departure, and perhaps few people really knew how long an apparently new innovation had been maturing in his mind and prayers before it was presented as a fully fledged plan. He had in abundance that mixture of sagacity and enthusiasm which knows how to look before you leap as well as to strike while the iron is hot, and he sought for the same qualities in those who worked under him. To approach the Bishop with an undeveloped, visionary scheme, its practical applications still indefinite, was to court a merciless exposure of all its probable snags. To take the bit between your teeth and start off without his blessing was to risk, at the very least, a thorough-going snub! But to ask his counsel for a plan, well conceived and carefully thought out, was a sure approach to sympathy and probably led, in course of discussion, to something far sounder and better than the original proposition. In the same way, he had little use for those who made mistakes by refusing to ask for help, but unlimited sympathy for those who would bring their difficulties along and ask for advice.

Meanwhile, the mass movement continued apace and was now crowned with a new and wonderful result. For the transformed lives of the Christians, working secretly as leaven in the villages, suddenly revealed the power to break down the age-long barriers of caste and bring the caste Hindus in considerable numbers to the Feet of Christ. The movement began with a general change of attitude and, as we have already seen, a growing respect for the Christian religion, as judged by its power to produce so notable a change in the lives of people whose complete degradation had always been accepted as inevitable. Then came a desire to know more of Christian teaching, even if it involved hearing about it from the village teacher of outcaste origin living among the untouchable community. The Christian women, too, found they had the entrée to the homes of the high-caste women, who keep a kind of semi-purdah, and more than once it was found to be the women who were exercising pressure upon their men-folk to embrace Christianity. The traditional respect for the Indian Guru was extended to the Christian Pastors, and the Bishop was continually invited into high-caste houses and treated as a deeply revered guest. Again and again, having placed him in the seat of honour, they would sit at his feet and beseech him : " Tell us about your religion." Then, suddenly, as if a pent-up stream had broken loose, something in the nature of a mass movement began among the Sudra castes of the villages. True to their ancient communal tradition, they came in groups, farmers, shepherds, potters, goldsmiths, etc., asking to be admitted to the Church and invariably giving as their reason for coming the change which they had seen with their own eyes wrought in the lives of the outcastes by the Christian religion. In 1924, at a baptism of 325 people only 25 were of caste origin ; three years later, in the same place, out of 117 people baptized, no fewer than 100 were drawn from various caste groups. The following day the Bishop held a Confirmation at which, for the first time, some of these Christians from the higher castes were admitted to full membership in the Church, one of whom said to him : " We were all waiting for this; there are 600 of our own people in 19 villages who have seen us and want to become Christians too."

By 1931 it was obvious that a new era had begun in the work of the Telugu Church. This movement, which had started in localized areas, was spreading rapidly from deanery to deanery. At first the baptisms had been chiefly among the ' border-line castes ', i.e. the lower grades of the Sudra hierarchy, some of which had once been wandering tribes and did not rank very high in village society; soon it was the leading castes of the village which were coming in considerable numbers. Moreover, there was no fierce outcry against them and comparatively little opposition. The old attitude of bitterness and aloofness on the part of the caste people had given way to kindness and genuine interest. As one Christian woman put it : " Formerly the caste people used to shout at us to get away if perchance we walked too near them; now all thought of uncleanness has disappeared. They do not mind sitting with us in church, touching us, praying with us to our Lord." Baptisms took place in which people from eight or nine different castes were baptized together with the outcastes. More amazing still, many hundreds were confirmed and received Holy Communion, sharing a common Cup with those who had hitherto been untouchable. Moreover, it was an undeniable fact that all this was taking place only in areas where there were keen Christian congregations among the outcastes. It was indeed one of the great miracles of the Holy Spirit at which all concerned could only marvel and thank God.

Needless to say Bishop Azariah was foremost in thankfulness and enthusiasm, for it was indeed the crowning

F

glory to the steadfast witness of countless sincere and humble Christians, which he had always maintained to be the most important instrument for evangelism. During these eventful years he was constantly in the villages, guiding and inspiring the clergy and teachers, meeting, with indomitable faith and courage, each new problem as it arose; blessing and encouraging, baptizing and confirming these new children of God, rejoicing in their great contribution to the Church of Christ. There were in truth many problems : the danger of their desiring the ministrations of caste evangelists; the difficulty of teaching large numbers of women who would neither come out to classes nor admit men into their homes; the multitudinous, thorny questions such as how far and how soon they must abandon social customs or taboos pertaining to their caste. Above all, there was the very real stumbling-block that almost all the Christian places of worship were in the heart of the outcaste hamlet, often close up against the houses of people whose job it was to slaughter animals. To ask high-caste Hindus to worship in such surroundings was to put too great a strain upon them; yet, "Live not where there is no temple " is a favourite Indian proverb which was often quoted by the Bishop as he urged the erection of new village chapels where they would be accessible alike to caste and outcaste, and churches of dignity and beauty which should be " sign-posts luring them to better things ".

But above all he rejoiced in the very marked gifts and graces which the Sudras were bringing into the Church. Reverence for the priesthood was already deeply ingrained; the whole-hearted and joyous observation of festivals was second nature; to bring offerings an accepted part of their worship. It soon became obvious that, in devotion to their new religion and respect for the ministry, in reverent worship and liberal giving, they bid fair to outstrip many of the older Christians. Their moral enthusiasm and fine spirit of sturdy independence were naturally a contrast to the low moral standards and the servile mentality that had been forced upon the outcastes for so many generations. Although they were not in any striking degree more literate, their level of intelligence and thoughtfulness was distinctly higher. Their courage in bearing witness to their own folk and their zeal in bringing others to Christ was second to none. Most surprising of all, their readiness to abandon caste privileges and repudiation of untouchability were more whole-hearted than anyone had dreamed possible. Without a doubt the Church had received a great influx of new life, fresh vigour and increased devotion with the adherence of these virile castes representing, as they do, the ancient yeoman tradition of rural India.

It was obvious that, as the mass movement grew and flourished, it must place a serious strain on the resources of the Church both in men and money. Not nearly enough teachers were available to meet the demands for new congregations. To refuse would-be followers of Christ seemed unthinkable; to withdraw teachers from the older congregations would inevitably lead to stagnation and the general decline in the quality of Christian life. At the same time it was apparent that the increase in the offerings of the Indian Church had nowhere near kept pace with that of its membership. In other words, the Telugu Church had not yet learned to give. Speaking on this subject at a conference in the Nilgiris, the Bishop began by saying that he stood condemned as a man who had failed to produce a ' giving ' Church, yet, driven by this conviction, it was exactly in this realm of Christian giving that, in the last years of his life, both by the written word and by force of example, he was to make one of his greatest contributions to the whole Christian community—for his book, *Christian Giving, a Series of Studies in Christian Stewardship*, has indeed become a classic. He began by condemning whole-heartedly self-support, " with all its ugly emphasis on *self* ", as an aim for Christians since, only too often, it began and ended with the support of the individual pastor by the individual congregation, leading to a narrow, selfish, parochial outlook and an unworthy conception of self-government. " ' He who pays the piper calls the tune ' may be a good slogan in mundane affairs, but it is unworthy as between Christian brethren." The inadequacy of Christian giving must be recognized as, *au fond*, a spiritual deficiency. " Christian giving is a religious duty; when man does not recognize God's ownership of his money, he has not fully recognized God's claim upon his whole being. . . . Where God's claim upon our money is ignored it becomes one of the greatest dangers to our spiritual life. . . . Christians must consider it part of their religious duty to give generously according to their power, yea and beyond their power, in order that the cause of their Crucified Lord may not suffer for want of money. If they are desperately poor they must give out of their deep poverty. . . . Christian giving *is* worship; offerings and all gifts must therefore be the expression of the giver's personal dedication to Him who bought us with a price and must be given in the spirit of worship. Church offerings should always be *offered* not *collected*."

The Bishop was not content to see this in terms of a shortage of money for God's work, but first probed it to its deepest spiritual foundations and then set to work, with his customary vigour, to practise what he preached. Many were the conferences he held with village elders at which he and they together reckoned up, item by item, just what it cost the average Christian family to live in food and clothing, house repairs, education (if any !), luxuries such as tobacco and bangles, and then faced the wholly inadequate proportion given to God. Many were the picturesque suggestions, gathered from others or devised by his own fertile brain, which found their way into his talks and writing. The handful of grain, put aside for God by each Christian woman every time she cooks; one chicken out of every brood, ear-marked for the Church; special thank-offerings on all family occasions, anniversaries, recovery from illness or confinement, the safe return from a journey, the calving of the buffalo, and so forth. At every service the offering must hold an important place. Large brass bowls or trays should stand about the church to receive the people's offerings in money or in kind and the act of consecration must be deeply reverent and worshipful. He waxed sarcastic over the Western practice of holding a bag menacingly before each member of the congregation and then offering unwillingly extorted threepenny bits to the Almighty, while the people were so absorbed in singing a hymn that they hardly noticed what was going on! Visitors to Dornakal Cathedral often remarked upon the solemnity of the moment when the entire congregation stood in silence while their offerings of grain, money and first-fruits of every description, followed by the Bread and Wine for Communion, were carried up to the altar and dedicated to God. Harvest Festivals, always a central feature of rural church life, received even greater emphasis. The annual Ingathering Services, held in every village, were often followed up with big central gatherings which, in course of time, came to be expanded into a mixture of the Italian *festa* and the Hindu religious fair. At Dornakal itself this was always one of the most impressive and homely of ceremonies, with its crowds of village folk carrying up the fruits of the earth, flock and farmyard, chickens, ducks, kids and calves (all alive!) while the Bishop, resplendent in cope and mitre, received and blessed their offerings. Then, with baptisms and religious drama, inter-village sports, singing, dancing and other competitions, the whole festival occupied a full forty-eight hours of glorious crowded life. By these and other means, in spite of war, failure of monsoons and famine conditions, the offerings did rise steadily year by year until it could no longer be said that the Telugu Church had not learned to give.

85

To see the Bishop at his best and happiest was undoubtedly to see him in the villages. Year by year his
Confirmation tours lasted from the middle of February
until the end of April in the steadily increasing heat, and
his report which followed indicated how much more than
the actual confirmations had occupied his mind. For
little escaped his attention. From the general spiritual
level of the congregation to the appearance of the smallest
child, from the progress of the mass movement to the
individual witness of the humblest man or woman, from
the largest issues to the most trivial details, everything
was noted and commented upon, praised and encouraged,
criticized or condemned. He was equally interested in
Christian or non-Christian, caste or outcaste, young or
old, men or women, and all were equally at home with
him.

He took immense trouble over baptisms and confirmations, anxious that an indelible impression should be made
on the minds of all who received these sacraments. More
and more he trusted the actual teaching required to the
clergy and spent his own time with the candidates in
testing their general degree of spiritual experience in
the Christian way of life, a somewhat hair-raising process
for those who had prepared them and did not know in the
very least what line of approach the Bishop might take !
Gone indeed were the days when any candidate would
begin automatically : " My godfathers and godmothers
in my baptism . . ." ! He was deeply appreciative of
genuine spirituality, however humble or unlearned, but
would descend like a ton of bricks on anyone who showed
blatant inattention or lack of interest. The services were
always deeply impressive and reverent, and a visitor
from England once commented to him on the splendour
of his full convocation robes, snow-white rochet and
scarlet chimere appearing suddenly from a temporary
vestry in a cattle-shed amid the drab dust-colour and
general unbleached appearance of an Indian village con-

gregation. " Yes," he said, " I want them to know something of the glory of the Church and how can they when most of them see nothing beyond the village chapel ? "

Perhaps one of his own best stories will bear repetition, for it gives a delightful picture of the Azariah of middle life and the happy informality of his life out in the villages. In the very heart of the mass movement area was a travellers' bungalow where he frequently stayed on his tours. Close by was the river, where literally thousands of people, drawn from many different castes, had been baptized. But in the neighbouring village there were no Christians. Several times they had given in their names, but, threatened with dire persecution from their landlord, had again withdrawn. One evening, walking back through this village, the Bishop and Mrs. Azariah stopped to talk with the women and were soon deep in a religious discussion. That same evening, after dark, the men of the village appeared at the bungalow to ask for baptism and a long conversation ensued. What had brought them to this decision ? It was the women, smitten to the heart by the words of Honourable Mother, who had made them realize their cowardice. The local Pastor was called, but appeared doubtful as to the genuineness of this sudden decision. The Bishop counselled time for thought, but the men were determined. So a pledge was asked for. The sacred lock, which every pious Hindu wears unshorn on the top of his head, should be cut off then and there and given to the Bishop in token of their sincerity. Mrs. Azariah then fetched her nail scissors, the bungalow watcher (a pious Roman Catholic) held the lantern, while the Bishop solemnly cut off the tufts and laid them in a sacrificial pile. Their persecution was long and severe, but a few years later the landlord himself came to the Bishop and offered, as a free gift to the Church, a valuable piece of land, only begging that a school and church should be built as soon as possible to produce more Christians of the type he had vainly tried to shake through persecution.

Thus the years passed rapidly away until Azariah had been Bishop for a quarter of a century and the Diocese prepared to celebrate its silver jubilee. January 8th, 1938, exactly twenty-five years since the newly consecrated young Bishop had been formally installed at Khammamett, was the date chosen for the celebrations at Dornakal. The water that had flowed under the bridge since then was indeed almost staggering. The small area then carved out of a corner of the Madras Diocese, had become a large bishopric, famous throughout the world for its courageous and effective missionary policy, its witnessing Christian community, its truly indigenous Church. The Christians, having nearly trebled their number, now totalled 220,000; there was an Indian ministry 150 strong; an Assistant Bishop had been found necessary to cope with the growing burden of episcopal responsibility. Above all Azariah had grown from the newest, untried member of the Episcopal Bench to one of the most trusted statesmen of the Anglican communion; from a coming figure in the Indian Church to the foremost Christian leader of India.

On the evening of January 7th, the railway station at Bezwada literally seethed with the faithful, clergy and laity, as the Grand Trunk Express was held up for three-quarters of an hour while they all attempted to board it for Dornakal. There tremendous preparations were on foot. The Cathedral, still alas unfinished, was to be used for the occasion and a temporary altar had been erected. The pervading note of the day, at the Eucharist, the special Thanksgiving Service and the common meal shared by all at midday, was one of family rejoicing and thanksgiving for God's blessing on the past years and God's gift of the beloved spiritual Father. Many were there who remembered the early years in the jungle at Dornakal and the doubts which surrounded the formation of the Diocese, and as the procession of all the clergy in their white robes, followed by the Bishop, entered by the west door and proceeded up the nave amid the great concourse of Christians gathered in from the villages, it seemed as if the very stones of the building must cry out in thankfulness for such a work, such a leader, such a blessing. And Azariah himself, what were his feelings? In the evening, after he had robed for Evensong and was waiting to take his place in the procession which was to chant a solemn Litany, he said suddenly : " Do you know the marginal reading in the Revised Version of Hezekiah's famous words, ' I will go softly all my days ' ? It runs : ' I will go as in solemn procession all my days.' That is what has been running in my mind all day; the obligation to go softly, humbly, as in a solemn procession of thanksgiving all my days, because God has allowed me to see this." Let us leave him there for the time being, his heart full of humility, thankfulness, joy at what God had done and he had been allowed to witness.

VIII. THE APOSTLE OF INDIA

IT has been said, with some truth, that there are only two subjects of vital interest to Indians, religion and politics, and that in India these two are one. At any rate it would be difficult for any patriotic, thinking Indian to remain wholly indifferent to the politics of his country, and the significance of nearly all political issues is to be found in the interaction of the various religions. What was Azariah's attitude to the ordinary political questions of his day? To answer a question so crucial and avoid misrepresentation, it seems best to quote rather freely from his speeches and writings.

In the first place, he was not a nationalist as that word is usually understood. He had, it is true, a deep love for India and a firm belief in her future, but always in relation to the Kingdom of God. He was fully alive to her weaknesses as well as her possibilities, and his own innate integrity and sense of justice forbade him ever to indulge in any form of self-deception or wishful thinking. Secondly, he had a far greater respect for the British administration in India, its law and authority, its attempts to maintain justice and equity, than would be accepted by the majority of his countrymen to-day. His personal experiences of England had been happy; he knew what Christianity in India owed both to the religious bodies of England and to the religious toleration established by the Government of India. He was, in fact, a patriot, giving justice where justice was due and loving his country with that fine discrimination that neither conceals nor condemns but seeks always the highest perfection.

At the same time Bishop Azariah could never be content with a general or superficial attitude, but must always weigh up any issue in the light of the Christian revelation. Consequently, on the comparatively rare occasions when he did deliver his opinion on political issues, there was invariably some fundamental question of human liberties or Christian principles involved. For instance when, in 1932, the Communal Award was published, the Bishop condemned whole-heartedly the proposal to have a Christian electorate, on the grounds that " it stamped the followers of Jesus Christ as a communal entity with distinct political interests of their own ". In an article widely published in the Indian Press he made clear his fundamental objections :

" The religion of Christ is one of the most dynamic factors in the world. It always bursts its boundaries . . . refusing to be confined to any one race, class or caste, seeking to embrace all. It is most true to itself when it refuses to be restricted by human fear or prejudice; if ever it becomes petrified or static it is dead. Thus the inclusion of Christians in a ' communal award ' is a direct blow to the nature of the Church of Christ."

He went on to point out that the award was bound to be a divisive factor among Christians, aggravating the differences which already exist, and prophesied that elections conducted on the communal basis were likely to plunge the Church into most un-Christian strife. But chiefly he foresaw that it would tend to separate them from the rest of the village. Already there was growing up a cleavage between Christians and non-Christians of the same outcaste community, since the latter were receiving special benefits from the Government, accorded to the Depressed Classes (as they were now called) but denied to their Christian brethren. In the case of the Christians of caste origin, now numbering some 25,000 all over India, their political and national cause was identical with that of their non-Christian relations who were fellow farmers or artisans, yet they were forced to vote in a separate constituency. "Thus a separation has been effected between the Christian Church and the country in general. We have permitted ourselves to be placed, not on the side of the whole community or nation, but on the side of a religious sect, a community which seeks self-protection for the sake of its own loaves and fishes."

As regards the Reforms themselves, and the measure of self-government they promised to India, he looked upon them with hope and confidence as a step in the right direction towards India's eventual freedom. In 1934, while they were still under consideration, a British M.P. wrote to the papers expressing the opinion that, under the new scheme, Indian Christians would be at the mercy of people opposed to the religion of Christ. Commenting upon this the Bishop said : " I do not know if there are many Indian Christians who, on such grounds as these, would look with disapproval on the new Reforms, nor do I think that anyone would like to see safeguards introduced to protect by legislation the rights of Indian citizens or missionaries proclaiming or following the Christian faith." He goes on to cite the native states of Travancore and Hyderabad as instances where large numbers of Christians have enjoyed the liberty to practise and proclaim their religious beliefs and then adds : " But even if this should be denied, Christians surely have enough faith in the truth of their religion and loyalty to their Lord to be ready to face persecution, or even death, for their Master. The Christian cause would certainly gain, not suffer, by such opposition." Thus he expressed in no uncertain terms his conviction that any political move which tended to separate Christians from the other communities, or give their interests special protection, was a denial of their true profession as followers of One who gave Himself for all.

Another point on which Bishop Azariah held very strong convictions was that the Church must ever be the guardian of ethical ideals, ready to challenge the Govern-

ment if it appeared inclined to compromise with a lower-
ing of moral standards in public affairs, and foremost to
support all efforts at social reform. As Chairman of the
National Christian Council for India he was ever alert to
see when and where this ideal could be implemented, and
sometimes carried more timid and hesitating minds along
with him on a wave of righteous indignation. Thus, one
of the last public actions he took, towards the end of his
life, was to protest against a proposal by the Central
Government to float a State Lottery in India, and he
quoted with strong indignation a statement from the
financial columns of a leading English newspaper to the
effect that such a method of national finance, while re-
pugnant to British ideas, was probably unobjectionable
for India !

He was always an ardent supporter of prohibition,
believing that most of the crime in the villages had its
source in drunkenness. " For over twenty years we have
made unrelenting war in the Christian community against
drink, and no one will deny that we can lay claim to a
great measure of success." Literacy was another great
aim for which he strove with all his might, but, although
by 1938 he could report that the Christian community of
India was twenty-seven per cent literate, he was never
satisfied with the progress made in that direction. Education, social uplift, economic advance, were not only
essential to the true life of the Christian community,
which must be wholly redeemed in Christ, but were
causes which every true Christian must have at heart for
the whole country and in support of which they must
join hands with any government that was prepared to
foster them.

" Many of us are true nationalists, in the sense that we
truly love our Motherland and have longed to see our
country placed on a path of progressive evolution towards freedom, enlightenment and united nationhood.
Any programme . . . with these ends in view ought to

have our hearty co-operation. Such are the attempts made by the present Government (the Congress Ministry of Madras) to attack the drink evil, rural indebtedness and widespread illiteracy. Our efforts to afford educational facilities to men and women, our leadership in introducing new methods for removing illiteracy, our ceaseless warfare on drink, superstition and debt are well known. Now that the Government itself is earnestly pushing these national services we ought to throw ourselves with them into these tasks that our ministry may reach not only the Christians but others also."

Thus he wrote in a charge to his clergy on January 6th, 1938, when the Government of India Act had just come into force, enfranchising one-tenth of the population of British India and setting up autonomous rule in the major Provinces. At this most critical point in the history of India he summed up his views on Christian citizenship as a whole with this appeal to the Christian ministry :

" The eyes of the whole world are upon Indian leaders. The success of the experiment will depend, not only upon the unselfishness and rectitude of the leaders, but also upon the spirit of service and fearless adhesion to the truth on the part of the elected representatives and the co-operation of the electorate. . . . You must lead your people to elect men, not of their own family or clan, but of undoubted ability, absolute rectitude, and genuine public spirit. If Christians will send such men to the legislatures they will make a contribution to the Government that can be made by no one else."

But the core of his belief regarding the political attitude of Christians went even deeper than this and may be found in the Report on Church and State which he helped to draw up at Oxford in the summer of 1937. Briefly it is this. Christians, by the very nature of their religion, must be law-abiding citizens, rendering unto Caesar the things that are Caesar's, and recognizing the State as an order within which Christians have to live and witness for Christ. At the same time loyalty to Christ must come before any other allegiance. This admits of no compromise, and on this point he was fearlessly outspoken in his warning to Congress leaders.

" Some leaders of Congress seem to be making the mistake of identifying nationalism with Hinduism. If the Congress Party allows itself to be suspected of such a narrow conception of nationalism it will undoubtedly bring upon itself the antagonism of the followers of other faiths. . . . Speaking for ourselves, our loyalty to our Master comes first, our loyalty to our Motherland second. We are first Christians, then Indians. We cannot, yea we dare not, acquiesce in any act of Government that interferes with our inmost sacred convictions."

Thus he believed and thus he taught that criticizing the State when it departs from Christian standards, permeating public life with the Spirit of Christ and training men and women to this end are paramount duties of the Church, while loyalty and obedience to the State as the guarantor of law and the servant of justice, are normally the duty of Christian citizens. *Disobedience may become a duty only if obedience would be clearly contrary to the Will of God.*

This all-important exception leads directly to his most notable contributions to public life made in 1942, when the Civil Disobedience Movement was rending India with the most bitter civil strife. The Bishop felt there could be no two views regarding the duty of Christians not to be associated with the excesses which were staining the name of Indian nationalism. However deep their sympathy with India's desire for freedom, whatever mistakes the British had made, for Christians to take part in mob violence and bloodshed was a denial of their higher loyalty as Christians. He fully recognized that this must inevitably lead to a state of tension in the minds of many Indian Christians between their double loyalty to their

95

country and their religion, but in the then state of Indian politics he could not see how that could be helped.

This statement, as might have been expected, drew considerable fire from some Indian Christians who accused the Bishop of defending the right of the State to exact an unquestioning obedience from the individual which bordered on totalitarianism, and declared that such sentiments, if true, would certainly lead many young Christian patriots to consider whether they could indeed belong to the fellowship of the Church on these terms. In his reply, the Bishop defined clearly the point at which, in his view, the Christian might be absolved from obedience to the State, namely, if and when the State tried to interfere with his religion. But he could make no concession with regard to the second half of the accusation. " If under these circumstances the inability of Christians to go the whole way with the Congress stumbles the young people and makes them indifferent to Church fellowship, I can only say I am sorry; but I am convinced that the Church cannot compromise its principles, even for the sake of winning these young people." And he summed up his reading of the situation thus : " It is my firm belief that, if we all can be uncompromisingly stern in our loyalty to our Lord, both the British Government and our Nationalists will alike recognize the reasonableness of our position as Christians. . . . I wish Indian Christian Associations all over India had taken a common stand on this two-sided loyalty. If they had done so they would have been a factor in the ministry of reconciliation which is so peculiarly theirs. Not placating this or that party, but speaking the truth in love will win respect."

Important as Bishop Azariah's pronouncements were, however, with regard to the tangled issues of politics and religion in India to-day, they were not his only, nor indeed his primary, contribution to Indian Christian thought, for his main interest lay in what should be the chief characteristics and chief contribution of Indian

Christianity to the Body of Christ throughout the world. "Give us a Church of India, a Church really our own, for which we can live and die," said Professor S. K. Rudra in 1915; and a non-Anglican Christian of Bengal once told the Bishop that, although greatly attracted to the Anglican form of worship, he could not belong to the Church of another country. "Call yourselves the Church of India and I will join you at once!" Thus it was with the greatest joy and hope for the future that Azariah greeted the disestablishment of the Anglican Church in India, whereby it gained its independence and became the Church of India, Burma and Ceylon. On this historic occasion, he was asked to preach in Calcutta Cathedral and there set forth his vision for the indigenous Church. First, it was not a new Church but one that was truly Catholic and Apostolic, preserving its ancient inheritance intact. "The faith delivered to the Saints, the Holy Scriptures, the Creeds of the Catholic Church, the Sacraments, the historic ministry, the worship and the rites of the Mother Church will be the heritage we shall continue to possess and use . . . conserving it to the peoples of India." The conception of the Anglican Church as a 'Bridge Church' between the ancient communions on the one hand and the younger free Churches on the other was one that especially appealed to him.

But there was also a unique heritage which, helped by this new-found freedom, the Anglican Church of India must increasingly make its own, the heritage of India's religious past. It could not be said that for thousands of years the people of India had sought after God for nothing. The numerous manifestations of the Spirit, loyalty in outward worship, reverence for sacraments, the capacity for sacrifice, attraction for the simplicity of the ascetic ideal, a mysticism which sees the Eternal in everything and longs for fellowship and union with the Supreme, all this rich harvest of religious devotion must be garnered and brought to the glory of Christ. "Chris-

97   G

tian Indians cannot cut themselves away from this
religious background. They must bring into the City of
God the honour and glory that belong to their national
heritage.''

At this time he also urged his clergy to apply this
principle in their own country, that the Telugu Church
might reflect all the valuable elements in the Andhra
culture, temperament and religion, consecrating to the
service and worship of Christ the architectural wealth of
the ancient cities, the artistic charm of Telugu prosody,
the devotional power and moral enthusiasm of the best of
their poets and writers. Likewise there were many traditional rites and usages which he regarded as purely Indian
(as distinct from Hindu) and these he desired to preserve
for the enrichment of the Indian Church. Worship before sunrise, the quiet hour for meditation at dawn, the
Indian posture for prayer or worship; the sanctifying of
all homely occasions, betrothal ceremonies, the entry to
a new home and so forth; the marking of special occasions
with special offerings brought to the Church for a special
blessing; all these and many more were things to be
welcomed and encouraged.

No one knew better, however, than Bishop Azariah that
the balance between traditional Christianity and progressive Indianization sometimes hung by a hair, and he
was adamant against anything that savoured, even re-
motely, of syncretism between the Christian and Hindu
religions. The modern tendency of some Hindu sects
which attempt to include Jesus Christ as a moral Teacher,
or even as worthy of worship, without giving Him the
supreme allegiance was anathema, and he would permit
of no compromise with picturesque ceremonies or festivals
which might tend to obscure, in the minds of simple
people, the dividing line between Christian and Hindu
worship. Long and vehement were the arguments he
sometimes had with Europeans whose ardour for Indianization often outstripped that of Indians themselves! He

knew the danger too well, and if, to the revolutionary, he seemed to err on the side of caution, to the old-fashioned and timorous he seemed bold in the extreme.

Perhaps the most interesting experiment upon which he embarked was a new Marriage Service. When the people of the various Sudra castes became Christians in great numbers they found the Christian marriage service very short and bare compared with their own lengthy and picturesque rites, and begged for something more sacramental and in keeping with the age-long Indian customs. In response to this demand the Bishop drew up a form of service into which he introduced several traditional Indian features. Thus the Sacred Fire, around which the bridal couple are accustomed to circle three times at the central point of their ceremonies, was replaced by a cross, standing about five feet high at the foot of the chancel step, and the bride and bridegroom were directed to walk three times round this, the most sacred emblem of the Christian religion, before making their vows. The marriage necklace of traditional use in India never has been displaced by the wedding-ring in the villages, but now this was to be blessed by the Elders, in token of their witness, before being consecrated at the altar. The bridegroom must then tie it round the bride's neck and make his vows with his hand resting on the knot. Finally, according to ancient village custom, the bridal scarf worn by the bridegroom was to be tied to the end of the bride's sari to signify the permanence of the marriage bond, before the priest pronounced the marriage blessing. A beautiful Litany and Thanksgiving taken from the marriage service of the Eastern Orthodox Church followed, and the whole made a most dignified and sacramental service of Holy Matrimony, in keeping both with ancient Christian tradition and Indian custom.

Undoubtedly the Bishop's most notable contribution to the Indianization of Christian worship, and the one with which his name will always be most closely associated, is the Cathedral at Dornakal. It was his idea that this great Mother Church should be a new departure in Indian Christian architecture, leaving aside the pseudo-Gothic, so dear to the Anglican heart, and the Byzantine, beloved of the Roman Church, but including the best-known features of Indian classical design. Above all, it was to be a building eloquent in its symbolism proclaiming to the non-Christian world around that in Christ alone is to be found the perfect fulfilment of the age-long search after God and Truth. The plan of the church as a whole was designed to harmonize with that of the South Indian Temple. The open space surrounding the church enclosed by a high wall, the deep porch through which the entrance is made, the tall towers flanking the western façade, the shape and design of the pillars are all well-known features of Dravidian architecture, but everywhere the dominance of the Cross makes clear for whom the worship is intended. For instance, the capitals on the pillars are of Hindu origin, showing a drooping conical bud from the self-propagating banana tree issuing out of an open flower of the *datura*, or deadly nightshade, signifying ever-continuing life rising out of death. By inscribing on these the Cross and the Lotus, the Christian sign of salvation and the Indian symbol of divinity, there is enshrined the symbolic representation of God who brings new life out of death through the Cross. Then again, the fact that the Cathedral is situated in an Indian State, ruled over by a Mohammedan prince, suggested the inclusion of Saracenic domes, once more surmounted by the empty Cross of the Risen, Victorious Lord. It is conceivable that æsthetically the combination of these varying styles is not perfectly harmonious, but there is no possible doubt that the Bishop's aim to make the Cathedral and its precincts a place of worship in which Indians should feel at home and thus be drawn to Him, who came not to destroy but to fulfil, has been amply realized. Witness the constant stream of visitors who love to wander in the peace of this holy place in the cool of the evening, or drop in to say a prayer on their way home from work.

The following incident will serve to show Bishop Azariah as the leading Indian Christian of his day, while pointing the way on to his supreme activity in the cause of Church Union. In 1935, Dr. Ambedkar, the now well-known leader of the Harijans, or outcastes of India, issued a famous proclamation in which he denounced the injustice of the caste system, cut himself adrift from the Hindu fold and called upon his people to follow him and seek their future outside. Enormous numbers obeyed him and there was a breathless pause in India while everyone waited to see what would happen next. Into which religious fold would they go? The answer on the part of their leader appeared to be : None. He made no further move. In various parts of India there were indications that some of these groups were drawn towards Christianity, but, since their motives were avowedly political, this was far from satisfactory. Eventually, Bishop Azariah sought an interview with Dr. Ambedkar and asked him plainly what his intentions were. Did he envisage any Indians, the most incurably religious people in the world, living without religion? Dr. Ambedkar's reply pierced the Bishop's heart like a sword. For, looking him full in the face, this is what he said : " I am well aware of all that the Christian Church has done for the outcastes of Hindu society. But at present we Harijans are one community all over India and our strength is in our unity. Can you in the Christian Church offer us any unity comparable to that? Have you one body that we can join as one people? " The only possible answer filled Azariah with such bitter shame and humiliation as he had never experienced before. For the One Body which is India's heritage had been denied her by the Churches of the West.

IX. THE PROPHET OF
THE WORLD-WIDE CHURCH

AND now to Union and so on to the world-wide Church.

It is June in Edinburgh, that lovely grey city of the north, so appealing in its austere beauty, so charged with the magic of its long eventful history, so potent to quicken the pulses and stir the imagination. Now, in this year of grace 1910, it is making history once again, but not this time for Scottish kings and queens, burghers and divines, but for the world-wide Church. Delegates from an infinite variety of Churches and denominations in all five continents, all of them deeply concerned in the evangelization of the world, are gathered there in conference, and among them a young Indian, who, as we already know, was destined to stir the still waters of Christian complacency and make for himself a name not soon to be forgotten. It seems incredible that only thirty-five years ago at such a gathering, out of 1,355 delegates, less than a score should be members of the younger Churches; yet so it was, and this fact alone lends considerable force to young Azariah's passionate plea for a general reconsideration of the relationship existing between them and the older missionaries.

"Edinburgh 1910" was a landmark in the history of Christendom, almost unparalleled in importance, because it marked the beginning of a new era in international and interdenominational Christian co-operation, and the means by which this has been achieved are the Christian Councils, now established in over thirty different countries of which India was one of the first. By the time the next Conference was held in Jerusalem in 1928 over twenty-five per cent of those attending were nationals of the younger Churches, sent by their own National Christian Councils, and the chief subject under discussion was no longer the missionary enterprise, seen from the angle of the ' foreign ' missionary, but the Christian message of the indigenous Church in its full application to all human relationships and especially to non-Christian systems of thought, which were approached constructively with a view to the evaluation of their importance in the development of religious consciousness. Could there be any shadow of doubt that Azariah would be in the van of such a movement? From the moment when John Mott toured the provinces of India, bringing with him a breath of the fresh air that had stirred upon the heights of Edinburgh, until the day of his death, Bishop Azariah was an indispensable figure whenever and wherever Indian Christians sought to promote co-operation and union among the Churches.

In 1929 Bishop Azariah was elected Chairman of the National Christian Council of India and never failed to serve it to the utmost of his capacity. Probably the most familiar recollection of him to countless Indian Christians will be in his white cassock and large amethyst cross, with his emphatic delivery and charming smile, presiding over innumerable meetings and conferences. He was a good chairman, quick to catch the trend of the debate, patient in allowing all to have their say, firm in applying closure when necessary, masterly in summing up salient points. When roused regarding a matter upon which he felt deeply, he could and did flash forth in trenchant criticism or strong indignation, and there were more than a few who, at one time or another, ' felt the rough side of his tongue ' ! If there was one thing he hated more than another, it was that anyone should come to a conference or committee with their minds already made up and a determination to ' get a thing through '. He often declared that for such a person to join in prayer for the Holy Spirit's guidance before the meeting was almost blasphemy and did he suspect anyone of such a design

103

they received short shrift ! During the intervals between sessions, or after the day's work was done, he was invariably to be found the centre of an eager group who were continuing with him some momentous discussion, drinking deep of his wisdom, enjoying his ready wit, marvelling at his extensive knowledge. It seemed as if he were literally untiring, since the end of the most arduous day of conference or committees found him still alert and ready for conversation, which with him, although sparkling and amusing, was never trivial.

A word must be said here of his capacity for friendship, for it is impossible to think of Azariah living or working in isolation. He was one of many groups, according to the wide variety of his interests, usually dominating, often critical, but always contributing something of value. On the Episcopal Bench in India, his first love and loyalty were given in generous measure to Foss Westcott, the beloved Metropolitan, under whom he served the whole thirty-two years of his episcopate. This great man gave Azariah his fullest support and co-operation in all his ventures towards the Indianization of the Church and in all his efforts towards Union, and their friendship was deeply rooted in mutual confidence and an unreserved love of India. Two other special friends among the Bishops were James Palmer, formerly of Bombay, and the late Harry Waller of Madras, both of whom were his close companions in the work for Church Union in South India. Azariah was deeply touched when Bishop Waller, a desperately sick man, chose Dornakal as the one place in India where he felt he could revive his weary spirit, and finally turned to him for help to face the bitter parting from India.

During his episcopate Azariah served under three Archbishops, Davidson, Lang and Temple. The first two, both considerably his seniors, were to him real Fathers-in-God for whom he had the greatest personal affection and veneration. There was also a special corner in his heart for Lady Davidson, that gracious hostess, whose welcome, on his first visit to Lambeth, remained an ever fragrant memory. With William Temple he had a deep affinity of spirit, sharing with him a common passion for unity and partaking of his vision for the world-wide Church. It was, in fact, those with whom he worked most closely in the cause of Union and in the great enterprise of missionary co-operation, who knew him best and valued him most highly. In India his partnership, as Chairman of the National Christian Council, with Dr. Hodge, for many years its Secretary, issued in one of the most notable friendships of Azariah's life. The Anglican Bishop and the Scottish divine were the firmest allies in countless Christian ventures, as tinder and flint to one another in conversation, and completely at home in each other's households. Study of the mass movement forged another intimate personal link with Bishop Picket of the American Methodist Episcopal Church. Names, past and present, come crowding to the memory; Posnett and Sacket, Banninga and Maclean, Rallia Ram, R. B. Manikam and many another. In truth they were legion, the leaders of the Churches, Indian, European and American, men and women of many denominations and various nationalities, who gave Azariah their confidence, acclaimed him their counsellor and were proud to call him their friend. For they recognized in him a man to whom the cause of Christ was infinitely greater than any divisions, an expert who gave freely of his own deep personal experience, a delightful companion, loving a good story, and taking his part easily and happily in any interchange of jokes and reminiscences.

It is obvious, however, that Bishop Azariah could not be content to stop short at friendly co-operation, however full and free, between the various Christian bodies of India. Such was good enough and vitally necessary in the absence of something better, but he could envisage the Will of God in nothing less than organic Union, and it was to this end that he gave himself patiently, hopefully, unstintingly for the greater part of his life and with which his name has become so intimately associated.

The beginning of the road is to be found at Tranquebar in the year 1919, when a group of Indian Christians met at the joint invitation of Azariah and the Rev. V. Santiaga of the existing South India United Church to confer and pray about Church Union. The Bishop himself has placed on record that they were all men with real sympathy for the deeper things of life, who had taken an active part in deepening the spiritual life of their respective Churches, having a common passion for the conversion of India, capable of great sacrifice, earnest prayer and steadfast action in winning India for Christ. They were convinced that only their connection with the older Churches of Great Britain and America was responsible for their divisions, and their aim in meeting was to secure an opportunity to discuss Church Union without the presence of the European missionaries. At the close of their meeting they issued an appeal to the Churches they represented to consider the question of Church Union, and from this humble beginning sprang the whole train of events which has led up to the proposal for a United Church of South India, so much before the public eye at the moment. The path has been a long and difficult one, going up hill and down dale, through bog and quagmire, over the heights of hope and down to the depths of discouragement, but although the star they followed has often flickered, by God's grace it has never gone out, and to many it has remained the brightest light in His firmament.

Briefly, the conditions of the proposed Union are as follows. The negotiating Churches, Anglican, Methodist, Presbyterian and Congregationalist (the last two being already in union), are all working in the Dravidian country of South India among a people united in race, social customs and cultural inheritance. There is little overlapping of territory, but constant travel back and forth and a good deal of intermarriage between the members of the different Churches. In the proposed Scheme of Union all these Churches have accepted the Nicene Creed as the basis of faith and the two Sacraments ordained by Christ Himself as being necessary to salvation. The form of Church government agreed upon is that of the historic episcopate with an episcopally ordained ministry, a great concession on the part of the Free Churches. But the existing ministries of the contracting Churches at the time of Union shall all receive equal recognition without further ordination, for a limited period of thirty years, an equally important concession on the part of the Anglican Church. Finally, there is a pledge, voluntarily accepted by all concerned, that, during the initial interim period, no congregation shall be forced to accept the ministrations of any man against their consciences until such time as there is a uniform episcopally ordained ministry throughout the United Church. As Bishop Azariah himself affirmed :

" We pledge ourselves, and fully trust each other, that in the United Church no arrangements with regard to Churches, congregations and ministers will knowingly be made which would offend the conscientious convictions of any persons directly concerned, or hinder the development of complete unity within the Church."

Thus the three main elements of the scheme are : first, the solid foundations of the historic Creeds, Episcopacy, an episcopally ordained ministry and so forth ; secondly, within the limits guarded by these foundations, a comprehensiveness within which all who are uniting can find a spiritual home ; thirdly, a frank recognition that union is a process in which there must be a place for both freedom and growth. It is based upon the principle that, in the cause of true unity, all parties have much to give and a certain amount to forgo, and upon mutual trust and confidence in each other's sincerity and goodwill.

Moreover, it has been deeply felt by all concerned that these are not simply pious hopes. During the years of negotiation, those who have regularly met together in consultation have passed through a deep spiritual experience in which they felt convinced that the Holy Spirit was leading them to a measure of agreement which, humanly speaking, had seemed impossible of attainment and which they longed to share with all other Christians. Again and again they came together to face an impasse which seemed hopeless; again and again, through prayer and deliberation, the way was made plain to full and frank agreement. It is in consequence of this common experience that they pin so much faith to the initial period of thirty years which is to provide the opportunity for growing together. " We recognize that this act of union will initiate a process of growing together into one life and of advance towards complete spiritual unity. If, during the process, difficulties and anomalies arise, the United Church must be careful not to allow any over-riding of conscience by Church authority, or by majorities, nor will it knowingly transgress the long established tradition of any of the uniting Churches. But we believe that these ends can rightly be attained, not by the forging of detailed regulations but by assurances given and received in a spirit of mutual confidence and love."

These proposals for a United Church of South India have been said to possess " the broadest range, the most original and daring form and the most definite detail " that have yet been shown in the realm of Church Union. Whence came the momentum which produced this movement, carried the negotiations so triumphantly over so many stumbling-blocks and kept alive the will to unite through so many years of hope deferred? Bishop Azariah has defined it in several great speeches, at Lausanne in 1927, at Lambeth in 1930, at Edinburgh in 1937. Again and again he appeared at these big Conferences of the

Anglican Communion, or the world-wide Church, as the great protagonist of Union, setting forth a vision that went far beyond a mere healing of the breaches between Anglican and Free Churches, looking towards an all-embracing union in the spiritual realm to match the new unity that twentieth century science has brought to the physical world.

It was his firm conviction that South India had been given a peculiar responsibility because of certain unique conditions which made Church Union both more imperative and more possible there than in many parts of the world. In the first place, there is the background behind the Church of people springing from a common racial stock, with a common social heritage and a common culture. Faith, patriotism, social customs all unite them; only the Church divides, with the result that, to the young Christian patriot of South India, spiritual fellowship with his fellow-countrymen is a living reality, whereas participation in a common Sacrament with his fellow-Christians is an impracticable ideal. Secondly, there is the situation within the Christian community, which contains representatives both of the earliest Christians in India and the newest congregations; members of the ancient Syrian Church, the Anglican Communion, the reformed Churches of Luther and most of the more modern Protestant off-shoots both in America and Great Britain. Imagine the absurdity of a young Indian, on being asked to what Church he belongs, replying : " I am a Canadian Baptist," or " a Swedish Lutheran " ! Yet for hundreds and thousands of Indian Christians all these differences exist not in matters of theology, but for reasons of geography. What Church you belong to is merely a matter of where you are born; what you are by conviction is quite simply a Christian. Consequently, the thinking Indian feels, and feels bitterly, that he has inherited willy nilly a system of divisions which he did not create, does not want to perpetuate and which do not touch his deepest experience.

Thirdly, there is the presence of the non-Christian world around the Church and the forces arrayed against it. The urgent question for Christians of all denominations is not : Which rule ? i.e., Episcopal, Presbyterian, Congregational etc., but : Whose rule ? i.e., Christ's ? or not Christ's ? The feebleness of Christian witness, the stumbling-blocks put in the way of would-be believers, the incalculable loss sustained in a caste-ridden country like India by the sin of a divided Christendom can never be exaggerated and have led to a passionate demand for Union.

" We must have *one* Church, a Church of India which can be our spiritual home, where Indian religious genius can find natural expression, a living branch of the Holy, Catholic, Apostolic Church, the visible symbol of unity in a divided land, drawing all men to our Blessed Lord. . . . Unity may be theoretically desirable in Europe and America; it is vital to the Church in the Mission field. Divisions may be a source of weakness in Christian countries; in non-Christian countries they are a sin and a scandal."

Thus Bishop Azariah laid before his own Communion and the world-wide Church his own burning convictions and those of his countrymen regarding the bitter evils of disunion, and appealed with all the eloquence in his power for the will and desire to unite. He realized, none better, that no union would be possible or worth having in India unless it radically altered the relations of similar Churches at home. " No happy home is possible for a young couple if their parents are not on speaking terms ! " But he also made it abundantly clear that far above any practical considerations of the weakness in the Church caused by the dissipation of its forces, or the harm done to the world by the spectacle of Christians worshipping in separation, he placed the bitter hurt caused to our Lord by the rending of His sacred Body. For this reason all approach to union must be through repentance.

" The cost (of union) is penitence and sorrow for our

share in the divisions, a true repentance that will make amends for the past by willing acceptance of necessary adjustments, a determined will to discover the way of union, agonizing prayer that the High-priestly interces- sion of our Lord may be answered, dedication of all our knowledge, possessions and prejudices to promote this cause. Are we ready to pay the price ? "

That the chief fault lay with the older Churches no one could deny, and Azariah was at once too loyal an Anglican to dissociate himself completely from their responsi- bility and too sincere an Indian to fail his own countrymen over this tremendous issue. " Speaking as a son of one of the younger Churches to our fathers in Christ in the older Churches I wish to say : We thank you for this ministry and we thank God for you. Your children by millions in every quarter of the globe rise up and call you blessed. But we wonder if you have sufficiently contemplated the grievous sin of perpetuating your. divisions and denominational bitterness in these your daughter Churches. . . . We want you to take us seriously when we say that the problem of union is one of life and death with us. Do not, we plead with you, do not give your aid to keep us separate, but lead us to union so that you and we may go forward together and fulfil the prayer, ' that they all may be one '."

Thus Azariah pleaded before the world this cause that was dearer than life itself and, in 1930, he travelled to Lambeth to sponsor the scheme before the assembled Bishops of the whole Anglican Communion. At the out- set there were many who would have liked to postpone the whole issue, but, as the days passed, it was apparent to all that the Holy Spirit was leading them out to a new and far wider view of Church Union than had held the field hitherto. The final proposal that the United Church of South India, when it came into being, should not be an integral part of the Anglican Communion, but would eventually, it was hoped, be in Communion with the Anglican Church, provided a solution which was accepted unanimously with deep thankfulness for the part that Indians seemed called to play in this wider vision of a more comprehensive unity, and with one accord the Bishops stood to sing the Doxology. What it meant to Azariah at that supreme moment that his brother Bishops of his own beloved Church should give no niggardly approval, but their whole-hearted blessing, to India's highest aspirations no words could express. In a moving little speech he begged that Lambeth should bid them Godspeed but not good-bye, representing the decision not as a schism but as a separation for a time in the interests of a greater reunion to be consummated later.

Would that the story could end there, but, alas, the years since then have been full of hope deferred, niggling alteration and hardening opposition. By 1935 the Bishop was writing : " I cannot help feeling that we are wasting too much time in perfecting the scheme on paper, while by this very work we defer even the beginnings of actual union indefinitely. We have come to love this literary work so greatly . . . that I fear we shall be sadly disappointed when the work comes to an end and the Union is actually inaugurated ! . . . I am inclined to cry : What does it matter ? . . . When the literary language is perfect and every whit satisfactory, is that the Union of our ambitions, our prayers, our efforts of the last fifteen years ? Should we not cease from wasting time in perfecting this compendium of united theology and do what is necessary to launch union itself ? " This is indeed the cry of a man who is sore at heart over the restricted vision and meticulous criticisms of lesser men. No doubt there were some who felt that he would have risked too much and ventured too far in his sublime faith in the goodwill of his fellow-Christians, that he underrated the force of the objections that were being raised, that he had scant sympathy for the quite honest doubts and fears of the extremists on either side. Be that as it may, there

can be no doubt that the atmosphere surrounding the
negotiations did change from the pure breath of mutual
trust and eager desire to the miasma of suspicion, mis-
understanding and obstructionist tactics. Small wonder
that, remembering the glory of the dawning vision, a man
like Azariah should feel sick at heart. And that this
feeling was shared by many another Indian is plain from
the very poignant appeal to the Western Churches which
went forth in 1936 over the names of twenty-two leaders
of Indian Christianity, pleading for help and sympathy.
" Union is a matter of life or death to us, yet the leaders
in the West speak lightly and say : The time for union is
not yet. . . . Would you then say that we should not seek
union among ourselves if we desire to be in fellowship
with you ? " The road which started so long ago in
Tranquebar had indeed proved to be the way to Calvary.

So we come to the winter of 1938-39 when it seemed as
if the various strands of the Bishop's life converged and
met in a most wonderful climax. The World Missionary
Conference met at Tambaram, the lovely new home of
the Madras Christian College. The younger Churches
provided fifty per cent of the delegates, one-third of whom
were under thirty-five. The theme of the Conference was
the Church, its faith, its life, its witness, its environment.
During the thirty years which had elapsed since the
meeting at Edinburgh the whole emphasis had shifted
from mission to Church, from evangelization by a foreign
agency to the witness of indigenous Christians. Here,
indeed, Azariah was on his native heath. To members
of the Conference he was one of the giants of old whose
name had long since become a legend ; he was one of the
architects of the world-wide Church ; he was the acknow-
ledged leader and elder statesman and yet so completely
accessible to one and all ; he was the genial host welcoming
old friends and new to his beloved India. He spoke on his
favourite theme, the Church and its witness, with all the
telling story of Dornakal behind him, and delighted his

audience with his shrewd thrust : "Too much of the
energies of ministers and the Church is being spent on
taking permanent care of hereditary Christians !" He
celebrated the Holy Communion on Christmas Day, and
surely there had never been such a gathering in of all
races and denominations at the Lord's own Table on the
Lord's own Birthday. And then he hastened back to
Dornakal to prepare for the Epiphany festival which was
to see a veritable manifestation of Christ's glory in the
Consecration of the Cathedral.

For at long last it was finished, thanks, in the final
stages, to the generosity of friends in America, and
Dornakal was preparing to welcome enthusiastically all
who wished to join in her joyful celebrations. And indeed
there were many. Old friends from Tinnivelly, who
remembered the early days in the old brewery; the clergy
and laity of a now world-famous diocese; Indian Christians of every denomination; representatives of the
Church from far-flung corners of the world; Bishops from
all the five continents, European, American, Indian,
African and Maori. And to each and all Azariah was a
household name and a beloved friend. The building had
made such rapid strides during the past year that it
seemed nothing but a dream to those who had watched it
grow through the interminable years. Yet there it stood,
this fair Temple of God, its twin towers soaring up and
up, its snowy domes with shining silver crosses gleaming
against the incredible blue of the winter sky. Inside, all
was cool and restful, with wide doors standing open to
deep verandas, and a subdued light filtering through the
pierced stone of the clerestory on to the great expanse
of polished floor. The furnishings, few, simple and dignified, were all gifts, many of them made in the Dornakal
workshops, and thus it might almost be termed a home-
made and hand-made cathedral since every stone had
been chiselled, carved and lifted into place by the united
efforts of the gipsy men and women whose pride in the

finished building certainly equalled that of the Bishop!

The Consecration day opened with a touching little ceremony when the people of Dornakal went by themselves to say good-bye to the little old church of so many moving memories. Then followed the great procession of clergy and Bishops round the outside of the Cathedral precincts, chanting the Litany and Psalms of Ascent in Telugu lyrical form.

" Lift up your heads, O ye gates, and be ye lift up, ye everlasting doors, and the King of Glory shall come in."

So the great congregation, waiting inside in a crescendo of tense expectation, heard them approach, stood in breathless silence while the Metropolitan unlocked the great west door, and then fell on their knees as he stepped over the threshold. A long and elaborate ceremonial followed in which each of the nine Bishops took a separate part in the Consecration, and finally the Eucharist was celebrated and nearly two thousand people received Communion where thirty-five years before there had not been a single Christian. Surely there was manifested on that day, and in that Cathedral, the three things for which Dornakal and Azariah have ever stood; the evangelistic fervour of a witnessing Church, the beauty of the Catholic heritage in faith and worship, the glory that India can bring to the unsearchable riches of Christ. When the setting sun dyed the great domes to a delicate rose-pink and the moon rose full and golden behind the hill, a tired but intensely happy company rose with one accord to sing, not the *Nunc dimittis*, but the *Te Deum*. Dornakal had reached a climax in her history; Azariah stood on the pinnacle of his life. But the glory belonged to God and His Kingdom must ever go forward.

X. FAREWELL

Eᴵɢʜᴛ months after the Consecration of the Cathedral the world was at war. India was directly involved from the outset by the Viceroy's declaration of war against Germany on her behalf, to which the Congress Ministers, then in power in six of the major Provinces, took great exception on the grounds that it was an arbitrary act upon which Indians had not been consulted. Indian troops were sent overseas and appeals were made by the Central Government for men and money towards the successful prosecution of a war which had been denounced by the Congress as imperialistic and in which they refused to co-operate. After several months of strained relations between the Provinces and the Centre, the Provincial Ministries resigned, their functions were' taken over by the Governors and the political deadlock continued for the remainder of the war. Bishop Azariah had scant sympathy with the Congress attitude. To him the fundamental issue of the war was clearly a moral one in which was involved the destruction or survival of the everlasting ideals of justice, freedom, righteousness and truth. For Christians to stand aside or even to show hesitation in praying for victory seemed to him to be a negation of their deepest convictions.

The earliest repercussion of the war on the Church of India came with the internment of the German missionaries in September 1939. This was followed, in the summer of 1940, by the complete isolation of the Danish Mission, the earliest branch of the reformed Church to be established in India, from its main source of supply in Denmark. The Christians of India were called upon to shoulder this new financial burden and, as Chairman of the National Christian Council, the Bishop was largely responsible for seeing that the spiritual, educational and philanthropic work of these missions did not suffer eclipse for lack of funds. During those anxious days when the world reeled under the shock of the German advance, country after country falling like ninepins until the Nazis obtained such a stranglehold upon Europe that it seemed but a step to the domination of the world, Bishop Azariah wrote a letter to his Diocese giving clear directions on what he believed to be the duties of the Church at this crisis in world history. These were, to have absolute faith in the sovereignty of God no matter what happened; to spend and be spent in unremitting prayer, personal service and sacrificial giving; above all to uphold the banner of Christ and press forward with the work of evangelism that their witness to the eternal values might neither flag nor cease though all the world might seem to deny them. Night after night at nine o'clock the great bell at Dornakal rang out to remind all within reach of its sound of the hundreds of thousands who were fighting, suffering, dying in the cause of freedom, and it was a solemn experience to gather with the faithful in the dim light of the Cathedral and to realize how strong were the bonds which united them to Christians they had never seen in countries they had but heard of.

With the entry of Japan into the war in December 1941 this vicarious participation in its sufferings came to an end. From now on India was directly threatened and the long tale of disasters in the spring of the following year touched South India very closely. Both Tamils and Telugus are adventurous people, given to emigration, and there were large colonies of them in Malaya and Burma. By the swift advance of the enemy hundreds were cut off from all contact with their relations in India, and many lost their lives in the ghastly trek back from Burma through Assam to Bengal with the victorious Japanese army on their heels. Fear seized the Telugu villages and

rumours spread like wild-fire. Even at Christmas, six
weeks or more before the fall of Singapore, the Christians
in the villages around Dornakal refused to attend services
in the Cathedral because they had heard it was to be
bombed during the festival! By April the fear was
bordering on panic. The Bishop spent Holy Week at
Masulipatam, one of the possible landing-places for an
invading army, speaking day after day in a church
crowded with people whose hearts were failing them for
fear. The climax of his inspiration was a sermon on
Easter Day based on the twenty-second Psalm, a somewhat unusual text for an Easter message! But his
insistence on the transformation of suffering and despair
through the victory of faith was a wonderful tonic, and
many came away reassured by his radiant belief in God's
ultimate triumph. They needed such assurance, for a
week later the threat of invasion was imminent, and the
people of Masulipatam were ordered to evacuate at a
moment's notice. In the general *sauve qui peut* up and
down the coastal area which followed not one Christian
Pastor left his post; all obeyed the Bishop's orders and
remained with their people.

Writing shortly afterwards, when, for the time being,
the scare had subsided, the Bishop quoted Isaiah's words
written under similar circumstances : " In quietness and
confidence shall be your strength," and added : " I
earnestly hope our clergy and Christian workers will become embodiments of that quietness and confidence which
comes through trust in God. Surely we Christians ought
to be models of fortitude, courage and strength because
we believe in God . . . and can interpret to the common
people the issues of the war and the purpose of all
suffering."

The war in the Far East stimulated recruitment among
young Indians considerably, and brought new problems to
the Church in that many of its younger generation had
left the villages and were scattered throughout India in

the forces. The Madras Presidency held a high record in
the number of its volunteers and among them Telugu
Christians were well to the fore. The Bishop took infinite
pains towards providing spiritual ministrations for
Indian Christians who were serving their country, and
released several Indian clergymen from his Diocese to
work with the Army Chaplains. On one occasion, when
away on his holiday, he was approached by a group of
Telugu sepoys with a request for Telugu Bibles, prayer-
books and hymn-books. He then found to his great joy
that they were holding prayers every night in a small room
which had been placed at their disposal by their Com-
manding Officer. Three times the Bishop drove a considerable distance to visit them, and finally conducted
a baptismal service in Telugu in the garrison church for
a soldier who had been brought to Christ by this little
group. Such an incident as this, together with the very
high tributes paid by many of the Army Chaplains to
the character and witness of the Indian Christians in the
forces, were a cause for deep thankfulness, proving, as
they did, how strong was the hold of the Christian religion
on many of the younger generation.

The war certainly did nothing to diminish the demands
made upon the Bishop, but in spite of the difficulties it
created, it was during these last few years of his life that
he saw the fruition of some of his most cherished hopes.
One of these was a notable step forward in the evangelization of India by Indians. In 1860 the C.M.S. had started
work among the Gonds, an aboriginal people living in a
remote part of the Central Provinces, but now, after
eighty years, lack of money compelled them to give it up.
In their straits, the society appealed to the Christians of
South India to take on this added responsibility for their
own countrymen and it was accepted jointly by the
Dioceses of Madras, Tinnivelly, Travancore and Dornakal.
Men and money were quickly forthcoming and Bishop
Azariah threw himself whole-heartedly into the project,

providing special training at Dornakal for the new missionaries and going himself frequently to give advice on the spot. It was a source of great satisfaction to him, both that a missionary society should turn to the Indian Church for help and that Indian Christians should have responded so promptly to the call, and his personal happiness in this new venture was increased by the fact that his own daughter, carrying on the family tradition, was among the first Indian missionaries to the Gonds.

The crisis which developed when the Japanese threatened invasion, had made it necessary to take stock of the extent to which the Church in India still depended upon the presence of foreign workers. In the event of all the British and Americans being rounded up into internment camps, could the Church have carried on without them? Undoubtedly the institutions might have suffered considerably, but the pastoral work, at any rate as regards the men, would have carried on with little or no change of personnel. Work among women, however, would have been seriously hampered, since there had been no supply of educated Indian women offering for Church work as there had been in the fields of education and medicine. It was therefore a great relief to the Bishop when, between the years of 1940 and 1942, three young women of higher education and considerable teaching experience offered themselves for pastoral work among Christian women, and the personal care he lavished upon every detail of their training showed how much store he set by this new development. They were commissioned for service in the Cathedral at Dornakal by the Bishop himself, only a few months before his death, and the great responsibilities he laid upon them, in giving them the supervision of practically all the work among women and children in some of the largest mass movement areas, showed the extent to which he trusted and believed in them.

It was no new departure for Azariah to show an interest

in women's work. " No congregation is better than its women " was one of his maxims, and he was always ready to give of his best to study schools and conferences for the women of the Diocese. He encouraged the appoint- men of Women Elders, directing that places should be found for them on the village Councils of Five when a case concerning a woman had to be tried, and more and more he desired to make provision for women in the councils of the Church. Women's education was a cause very dear to his heart, for he knew that only a steady supply of consecrated women leaders with a strong sense of vocation could meet the needs of the Christian com- munity now and in the years to come. Moreover, such women were needed not only to lead and to educate, but also to keep the homes and bring up the children of the Christian Church. In these later years, he became very concerned about the sexual problems and low moral standards prevalent in the villages and tackled the subject himself in direct fatherly talks to clergy, teachers and women workers, begging them to be equally frank with the young people. His book on Christian Marriage em- bodied much of this teaching, and he was certainly ahead of his time among most of his compatriots in his views on the subject of sex-education.

Above all he was concerned with the fact that the Telugu Church had entered upon a new phase in which the care of Christians of the second generation presented new and special difficulties. In 1941 there was celebrated at Masulipatam the centenary of the arrival of the first missionary from England. In the place where Robert Noble had toiled for years, at first making hardly a con- vert, thousands of people had assembled to do honour to his memory. At the Communion Service, the faithful knelt right across the wide church from the end of one transept to the other and, even with sixteen priests assist- ing, the administration alone took nearly an hour. The average of the oldest congregations was eighty years; of the total, about a quarter were sixty years old and up-wards, the remaining three-fourths, hardly forty. Al-though the Church was still growing steadily, the majority of its members were now no longer those who had experi-enced the thrill of turning to Christ, but those who had been born into the Christian fold, a fact which created wholly new problems.

The Bishop's charge to the clergy in 1941 showed how greatly these difficulties claimed his attention. In it he set forth plainly both the advantages and drawbacks with which they had to reckon. " This is a new generation to whom idolatry and superstition are foreign. It has inherited a certain degree of Christian civilization and has tacitly accepted a certain standard of ethical conduct. . . . Yet this very achievement may make it oblivious of that personal experience of forgiveness of sin and new life which marks the regenerated man. Further it is a generation which has grown up in a Christian atmosphere, under the sound of the church bell. . . . The bare facts of our Lord's earthly life are common knowledge . . . yet the deeper meaning of these facts . . . is to a great extent unknown or at least has not been assimilated in life. Familiarity with truth is the danger. It is a generation that glibly makes profession of Christianity without necessarily realizing its obligations. The articles of the faith are taken for granted without examination and held without conviction. Again, it is a generation of men and women who have inherited a freedom which perhaps in its turn has brought in secularism and materialism, which are apt to choke the life of Christ . . . and often results in behaviour which is far from the Christian ideals of humility and love. Irresponsible and ignorant criticism of the Church and its ministry may be among its character-istics; forsaking the assembling together for worship and participation in the Sacraments may become its custom." The Bishop was looking ahead, anticipating results which he knew would follow the tendencies he discerned, uttering grave warnings to clergy who were often bewildered by this new trend of events. Members of all Churches in this country, to whom his description will strike a note of terrible familiarity, will realize only too well the need of such a warning.

Yet to utter warnings without pointing to remedies was not Azariah's way. At this critical juncture there was no use in turning to St. Paul for guidance, since he and most other New Testament writers were addressing Christians of the first generation. It was to the Fourth Gospel, the Epistles of St. John and the Apocalypse that the Bishop directed the study of his clergy, and it was probably due to this that his own study of St. John's Gospel, assisted by the writings of Edwyn Hoskyns and William Temple, so filled his thoughts and coloured his teaching during the last few years of his life. The rich heritage of Christian worship and Sacraments, prayer and almsgiving; the deepening of faith and life through the mystical union with the living Christ; the steadfast witness of a holy community in a darkened world; these were the means by which God would perfect in the second generation the work He had begun in their fathers.

In August 1944 Azariah kept his seventieth birthday. It was a considerable age for an Indian, especially one who had lived so hardly and spent himself so unceasingly as he had. Yet to the outward observer he did not appear to show his age. Perhaps he was a shade less patient, less able to view with equanimity the frustration or postponement of his most cherished hopes, as in the case of Church Union. Perhaps he showed signs of flagging towards the end of a gruelling day of committees with the thermometer reaching three figures. Yet to all intents and purposes he was the same alert, shrewd, keen, enthusiastic servant of the Church, untiring in his efforts, unfailing in his interest. He had mellowed considerably since his early days, and his grandchildren could rush in with welcoming cries where his own children would perhaps have feared to tread except on tiptoe. They were all a great joy to him. His eldest son, Dr. Edwin Azariah, was in charge of a big L.M.S. hospital at Jammalamadugu where the Dornakal Diocese borders on to the London Mission area. The second son, George, was in Holy Orders and occupied a post on the staff of the Dornakal Divinity School, in daily contact with his father who depended on him more and more. Of the two remaining sons, Henry, after taking a post-graduate course in America, had returned to the staff of the Agricultural College at Allahabad, and Ambrose, the youngest of all, was in Government service in the Telugu country, while the second daughter, Grace, was married to John Aaron, a young Tamil priest working in the Dornakal Diocese. There were ten lively and attractive grandchildren who were a great source of interest and amusement in their frequent visits to their grandparents. The Bishop's holiday house at Kotagiri became a great rallying point for the family every summer, and in his comparative leisure from the more pressing day-to-day engagements (though his self-imposed holiday tasks invariably included the writing of at least one book !) they enjoyed more of his company than at any other period of their lives. Although the house was always full to overflowing, their hospitality was unfailing and there were many, Indians and Europeans, missionaries and others, who found their way to this lovely spot on the side of the hill with a panorama of the Nilgiris laid out before it.

Christmas Week of 1944 was spent in the village of Parkal, one of the most backward areas of the Dornakal Diocese, where the Church in Travancore supported two Indian missionaries. While combining a Christmas holiday with a visitation, the Bishop employed his ' leisure ' by translating, with the help of the Malayali missionary, the liturgy of the Mar Thoma Syrian Church and laboriously collecting statistics about Christians in various parts of the country from the latest census reports. He went from village to village, by bullock-cart or on foot, carrying out his usual round of pastoral duties, teaching, examining, confirming; rebuking the slack, disciplining the faithless, giving to many their Christmas Communion. On the last evening, walking back from a village at sunset, he met a young herdsman returning from his day's work and stopped to talk to him. "Are you a Christian?" asked the Bishop. "No," replied the boy. "Are there no Christians in your village?" "No." Immediately Azariah, the evangelist, sprang into action. "No Christians there? Why not?" "Because no one has told us," said the boy simply. The fire died out and an immense weariness came over the Bishop. No Christians because no one had told them! How could they believe without hearing, how hear without a preacher, how have a preacher unless one were sent, how send one when resources were strained to the utmost?

He returned to Dornakal on December 28th with fever, a not unusual occurrence which caused no alarm at first, but by the last day of the year he was obviously very ill and breathing with great difficulty. The following week was to be an important one for Dornakal since all the missionaries of the Diocese were coming for their annual retreat to be taken by the Bishop of Madras, who would also be the preacher at the dedication festival of the Cathedral on the Feast of the Epiphany. Bishop Azariah's mind was full of the arrangements for the hospitality of the visitors, never an easy matter in Dornakal, and he continued to think and plan from his bed when he was obviously too ill to do so. Yet, although anxiety was growing, even those nearest to him had no thought of imminent danger and the shock was proportionately greater when, on the morning of New Year's Day, the doctor who had been called in for consultation told them that he doubted if the Bishop would live for twenty-four hours. His constitution was entirely worn out by the pressure at which he had lived and worked for half a century and there was no power of resistance left. They tried to enforce the rest he needed so badly, but it seemed as if his brain could not relax from its severely disciplined routine by which every moment of his waking hours had been used in the service of his Master. Yet God was infinitely merciful in sparing him any long-drawn-out period of inactivity or gradual decline of power and energy. At midday on January 1st, within a few hours of the doctor's warning, Azariah slipped quietly away into the unseen, without any farewells even to those he loved the best, but with a look of such radiant happiness on his face as to swallow up all sense of loss in thankfulness for the triumphant home-coming of this good and faithful servant of God.

None of his sons were at home and not one of them received even the news of their father's illness until after he was dead. Many of the missionaries who had already started for Dornakal heard the news *en route*; some even arrived, knowing nothing, to hear the Cathedral bell tolling. All day long Christians and non-Christians alike streamed up to the Bishop's house to pay their last homage to Azariah, who lay in his robes in the little chapel at the corner of the veranda with that ineffable smile of happiness on his face that seemed to forbid all clamorous mourning. Indeed there was no wailing or lamentation in Dornakal that day. The superb courage and dignity of his nearest and dearest gave the lead, and never had the Mother of the Diocese been a greater source of strength and comfort to her children than in this her own hour of desolation. They laid him to rest as the sun was setting, in the garden of his beloved Cathedral, outside the east wall, immediately behind the altar, and as they carried his coffin to the grave they were singing, very softly, the Telugu Easter hymn : Victory to the Risen Lord.

There we must leave him, for the future alone can show the lasting value of his life and work. Three weeks after his death, the General Council of the Church of India, Burma and Ceylon gave their final consent, by a large majority, to the proposals for Church Union in South India. Like many a pioneer Azariah died in faith, " not having obtained the promise but having seen and greeted it from afar ". Yet was it perhaps a greater tribute to the silent pressure of his memory than if he had been there to plead the cause with his customary eloquence? He himself said once : " There are mountain-tops in every religion, Francis of Assisi, Mahatma Gandhi; but it is when a group of common men are changed that people see the power of Christianity." Probably the secret of his power was that he loved and believed in the common man until he made him believe in himself. He liked to call himself simply an evangelist, and to reckon himself as an ordinary man who had been enabled, by the grace of God, to do extraordinary things, while deep in his heart he hugged the knowledge : " By the grace of God I am what I am." Whether or not he will eventually be found on the mountain-top, one thing is certain : when-ever and wherever Indian Christians are gathered together for years to come, they will surely rise up and call him blessed.

INDEX